AF505865

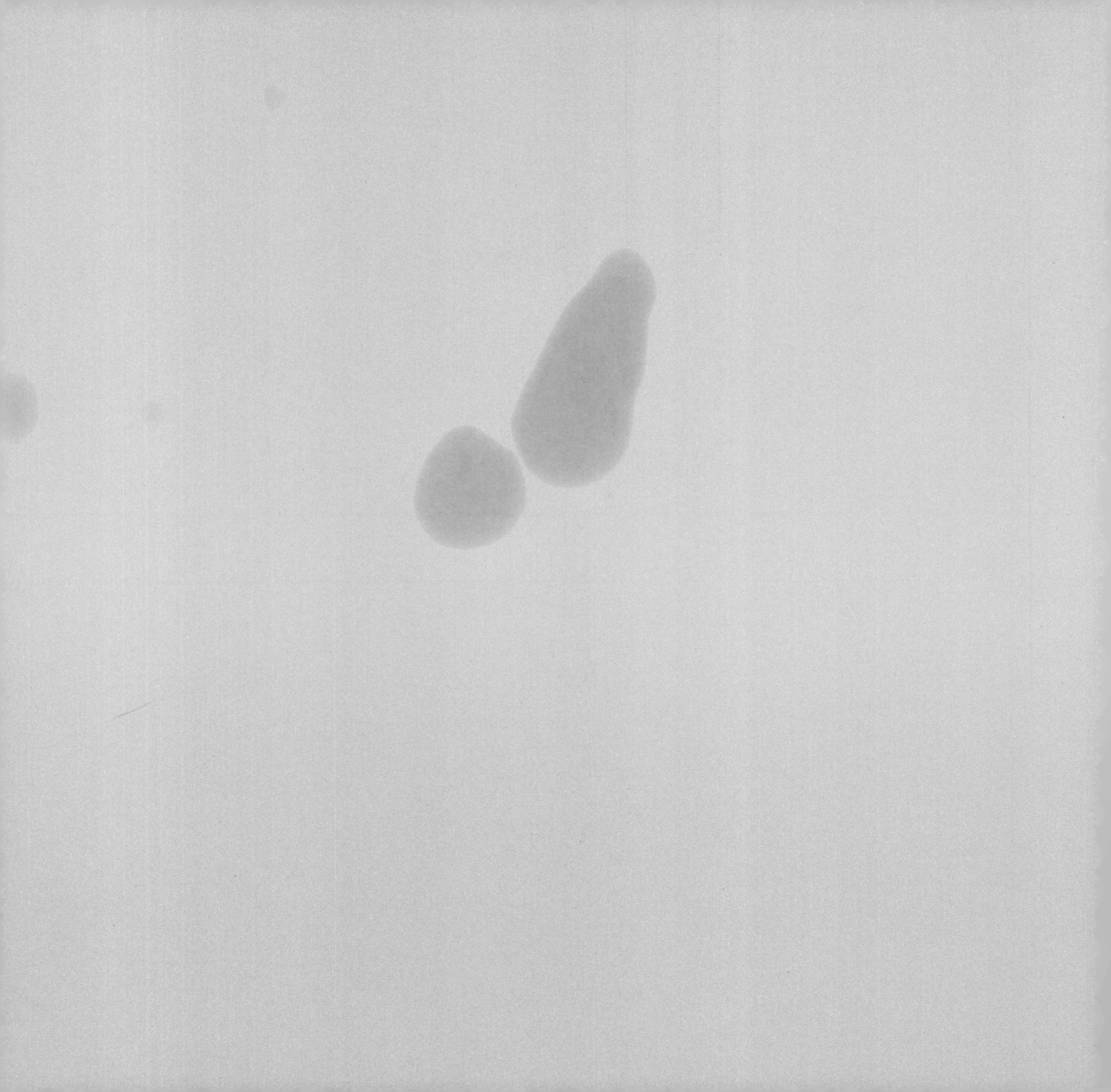

MÉNAGE

Beato

THE BETSY AND MARC ROWLAND COLLECTION

DRAWINGS BY BEATRICE WOOD

MÉNAGE: *Beato*

Text by Garth Clark
Photography by Addison Doty

Publisher
SF Design / Fresco Books
Albuquerque, New Mexico
frescobooks.com

Printed and bound in Italy
ISBN 9781934491560
Library of Congress Control Number: 2017907050

MÉNAGE

Beato

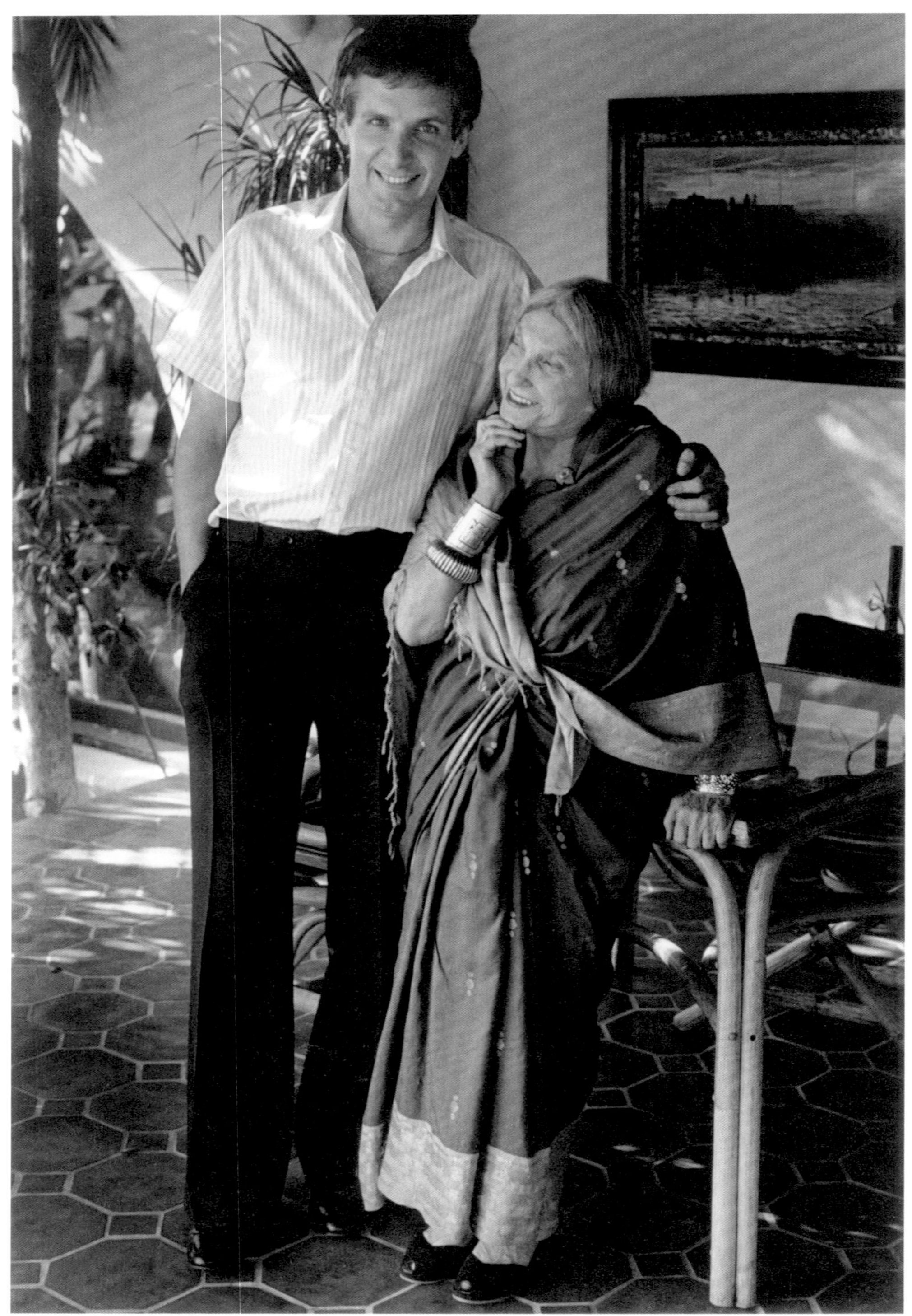

Garth Clark and Beatrice Wood, Los Angeles 1981.

INTRODUCTION

When you read about Beatrice (Beato) Wood (1893–1998) in the following two-part essay, it will come as little surprise that fifteen years ago a collection of drawings surfaced indicating that Jack Case (1917–1979) and Rhea Case (1913–2005), he, a photographer and TV producer, she, a journalist, TV personality and literary critic, had enjoyed a lively *ménage à trois* with Beato in Ojai, California, in the late 50s and early 60s.

Or, at least that is what the cards and drawings tell us. Some appeared to have documented events. Some might have shared fantasies. I have no idea which is which and it is not of consequence anyway. It is more about a state of mind, the courage to be free spirits, and not to be bound by the puritanical norms of society.

Beato was in her late 60's and early 70's when the ménage took place, which is remarkable in itself. It also contradicted the belief of some that Beatrice was all talk and no action. Clearly, there was action.

I want to deal with this delicately. Their escapades should not be read in prurient terms. All three players were deeply moral in their beliefs and were liberal, kind, and devoted to the development of culture and art. I will go a step further and say that Beato (as she was known to friends, though I preferred calling her Beatrice) was the most honorable human being I have known. She did what was morally correct no matter the cost to her personally and she was an unfailingly loyal friend and a kind, patient, and generous employer.

Thus, as we explore her sexuality as an artist, I want to emphasize that she was not promiscuous, she was liberated, two very different conditions. She had tried the former and did not enjoy the experience.

These texts will attempt to illuminate Beato and her views about life and art. There is no point in writing about the drawings… I know because I tried. I understand how fragile they are, not physically, but as the flickering, oblique capture of an event or as a delicious moment of erotica, real or imagined. So, I have left them alone to speak for themselves. As Robert C. McClure wrote in *The Grunting Determinate and Other Aphorisms of Robert C. McClure* (1978), "My art is like butter. If you clarify it, it loses its substance." Her drawings are eloquent and frisky, requiring us at times to lift skirts for the full impact.

This cache of gems exists only because of the perspicaciousness of the collectors Betsy and Marc Rowland. They were offered the collection when Rhea Case, now alone, moved to a home for the elderly. Several potential buyers had turned down the work, seeing the drawings and some ceramics as too ephemeral, too much of a sideshow. The Rowlands saw the value in a sneak peek into Beatrice Wood's life, her erotic spirit, and her Dada-like emancipation.

Without the Rowlands, this collection might have been lost or disseminated, and a delicious moment dissolved. Now they have taken this a step further by commissioning this book and donating its proceeds to the global ceramic education programs of the non-profit CFile Foundation. Their farsightedness and fondness for beneficial wickedness makes this book edition available to Beato's large audience, followers, and fans to come.

It begs the question, "What would Beatrice have thought?" You have only to read the titles of her own book to know the answer. She would have loved it. And perhaps there is no reason to locate that sentiment in the past tense. It is possible that Beato, who was always deeply spiritual and in touch with the world beyond, may be applauding right now. Even though as an actress she played virgins-at-risk (and was once one herself), she much preferred to be seen as a powerful, seductress who called the shots.

Garth Clark
Santa Fe 2017

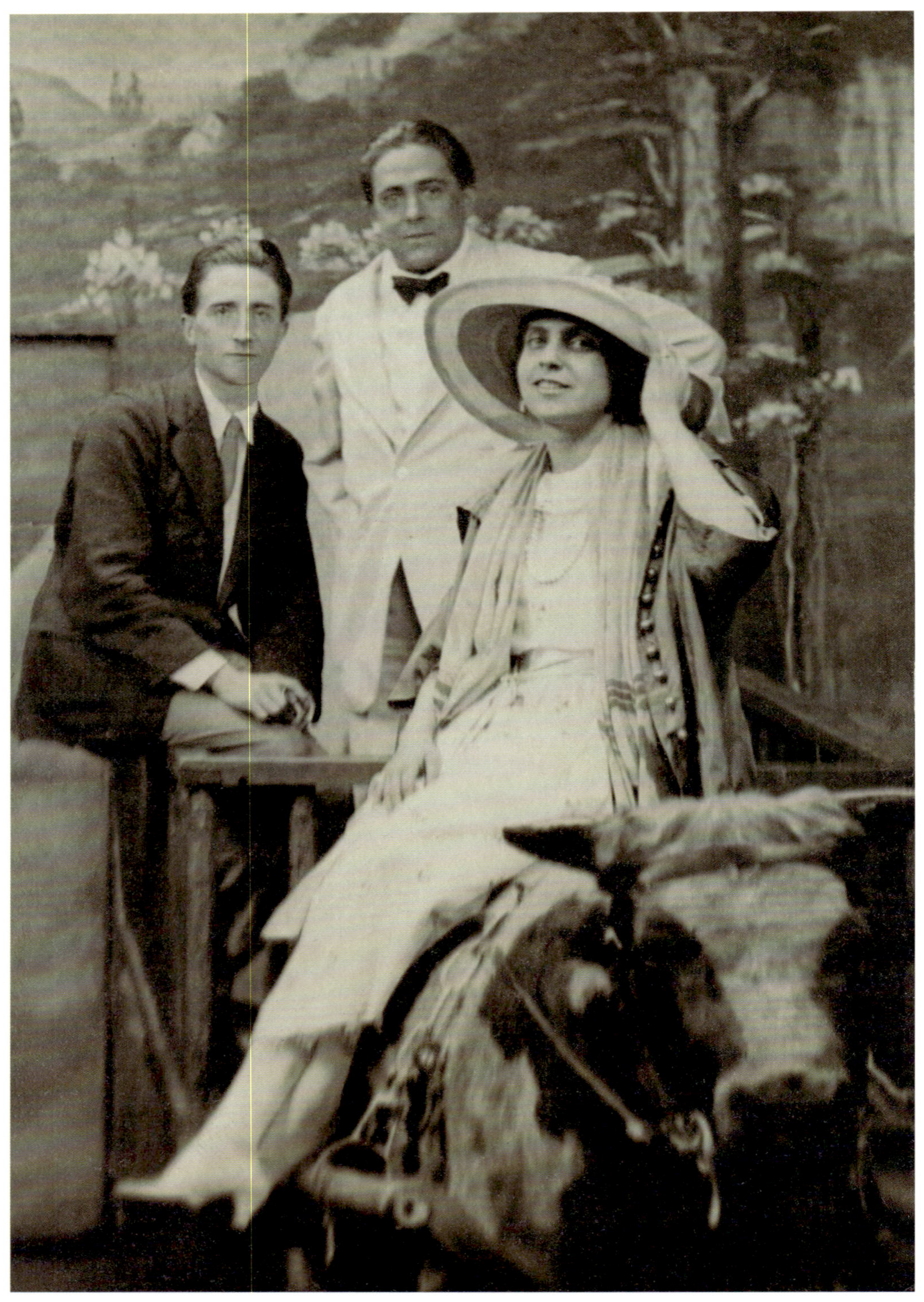

Beatrice Wood flanked by Frances Picabia and Marcel Duchamp in a photograph
taken at the Broadway Studios before their trip to Coney Island.
Courtesy Francis M. Naumann.

PART ONE: 1917 DADA

Beatrice Wood is the mistress of the *double entendre*.

If she were in a playful mood, her conversation would be laced with innocent words and statements that had a second, *risqué*, sexual meaning. And at times she would abandon subtlety and fling out an outrageous remark that left nothing to the imagination.

Once in the 80s at a luncheon I attended with the director of the Archives of American Art and the Director of the Delaware Art Museum, she grew bored with the conversation and with a twinkle in her eye volunteered why she was still so vital at her advanced age.

"Every night I leave my window open, and at 2am I have a gentleman caller." There were amused, patronizing smiles. "And his name is Major General Fuckwell." Knives and forks fell. She smiled sweetly and began to eat. That was the Dada in her.

She is known for her famous *bon mot* that the reason for her long life (aside from the aforementioned Major General, who was real by the way, but not the climbing through the window part) was "art books, chocolates, and young men." In the last decades of her life, Beato was surrounded by all three. She, and the young men who were drawn to her, developed lasting platonic friendships.

First, speaking for all Beato-lovers, our gratitude goes to Betsy and Marc Rowland—farsighted, adventurous collectors who saw the value in this cache of odd material far beyond any monetary worth. Not only did they acquire and present it, but in a double act of generosity on their part, they have funded this remarkable, exquisite art book, the proceeds from which will help fund the outreach programs of the Cfile Foundation.

Beato would have been indebted to them. After all, her autobiography was entitled *I Shock Myself*. And, perhaps, given the more spiritual, otherworldy side of her being, she is currently fully aware of this project, her eyes twinkling and with a smile of approval. The following anecdote will give an idea of why she would enjoy being revealed as a bohemian adventurer.

In 1917, having been introduced to the New York Dada group, Beato was walking with two Dada players, Marcel Duchamp and the Spanish artist Francis Picabia, at Broadway Studios before heading out to Coney Island. There they enjoyed an evening of fun, visiting sideshows and posing for a now very famous photograph. She was in high spirits, arm in arm with the two men when a policeman decided that she must be a prostitute and proceeded to arrest her.

For many women, this would have been a moment of degradation. For Beato, it was the finest compliment she had received in her young life. She was finally seen as a wicked woman, even a *femme fatale*. She was thrilled.

To understand this, one needs to consider her upbringing. Her father was a banker and her conservative mother only wanted to see her daughter presented to New Yok Society as a debutante. Beato always had to travel with a chaperone (for instance, when she moved to Paris to study art at the Académie Julian). And, her mother insisted that she be dressed by her maid every day until she was twenty-three. Beato felt stifled and repressed.

She was also naïve. Wood had little idea what being a lady of the night entailed—the drugs, alcoholism, disease, abuse, imprisonment, even murder and being the "property" of a pimp or a brothel, risks that defined their working lives.

To that end, Beato saw this profession through her own idealized prism such as in the upbeat, light-hearted manner of the musical *The Best Little Whorehouse in Texas*—a finishing school where young men came of age with mistresses of the erotic arts and where lackluster lovers could be re-educated in the skills of lovemaking to benefit, she always added, their wives and lovers. In a letter to Jack Case decades later, she objected to a book that painted a tawdry picture of the profession and bemoaned that the brothels of Paris has been closed down.

As a ceramist, she later made several large sculptures about Western brothels with the ladies hanging over balconies. Beato, inexperienced, conflicted, and often paralyzingly shy herself, admired their brazen directness and what she saw as their power in bed.

Now I return to the arrest on the boardwalk. The situation quickly became ugly. A Spaniard, Picabia's Latin blood quickly boiled over in response to this injustice to Beato's honor and was about to punch the policeman when Duchamp diplomatically intervened and defused the moment. They then continued their walk, with Beato on cloud nine because Picabia had been willing to fight like a knight for her.

The artist Joseph Stella later did the same, offering to fight a duel to uphold her reputation. Beato described Stella's bravery in a film shown at the Dada Ball that Mark Del Vecchio, my partner, and I organized. It was a giant performance piece for an AIDS benefit that brought out 1500 artists, club kids, and the drag community of New York. It was a re-creation of an event called The Blindman's Ball in its original 1917 venue, Webster Hall, which Beato had organized so long ago to raise funds for the Dada magazine *Blindman*.

In our contemporary version, Beato and Jasper Johns were the co-chairs of the Dada Ball. When asked to take on this role Johns replied, "How can I say no when a one-hundred year old woman invites me a to a dance?"

Sadly, Beato was ill for literally the first time in her life and could not attend in person but appeared on film, describing Stella's valiant offer, saying "he defended my," then looked a little confused, looked down between her legs, looked up, and with a wicked smile said, "my honor," to cheers and raucous howls of laughter from the attendees.

After the orginal ball ended at 3am, the party moved to the apartment of the collectors Walter and Louise Arensberg for more drinks and then upstairs to Duchamp's apartment where Beato, the actress Eileen Dresser, and painter Charles Demuth joined him to sleep in his small Murphy bed.

Squeezed into a tiny space between Duchamp and the wall, Beato later confided, "I could hear his beating heart and feel the coolness of his chest. I never closed my eyes to sleep." A few days later she memorialized the moment in one of her best drawings, *Lit de Marcel* (Marcel's bed).

1917 was a key year for Beato in throwing off the shackles of her controlling mother and becoming a member, if only by default, of the most avant-garde Dada movement—an anti-War, renegade intervention that changed art forever, giving art the power of concept over formal aesthetic values. It has roiled the arts ever since, both for better and worse, and this year, 2017, celebrates its 100th birthday.

Beato never claimed to understand Dada (few truly did) and would admit that she only ended up in this circle because she fell in love with two figures in the group—the writer, diplomat, and art collector Henri Pierre Roché, and Duchamp. Roché deflowered her, with great finesse, leaving her blissfully in love.

She imagined that this was the prelude to wedding bells and a house in the French countryside. However, those in the Dada group were not that conventional when it came to coupling as she soon found when Roché casually announced that he was sleeping with others as well. At that moment, she wrote, "The bowl that was my heart was broken, and laughter fell out." Then she met Duchamp and instantly recovered. She describes him as having the "charm of an angel who spoke slang."

They met at a duty call at the hospital bed of the composer Edgard Varèse. Duchamp was conversing with Varèse. Beato later wrote, "I became aware of a truly extraordinary face. He did not exhibit the hardness of a lifeguard flexing his muscles, but his personality was luminous. He had blue penetrating eyes and finely chiseled features. Marcel smiled. I smiled. Varèse fades away."

Some claim that there was a ménage between Roché, Beato, and the 29-year-old *enfant terrible* of the arts, as Beato writes,

> Roché had by now [1952] written *Jules et Jim*, later made into a film by François Truffaut. Because the story concerns two young men who are close friends and a woman who loves them both, people have wondered how much was based on Roché, Marcel, and me. I cannot say what

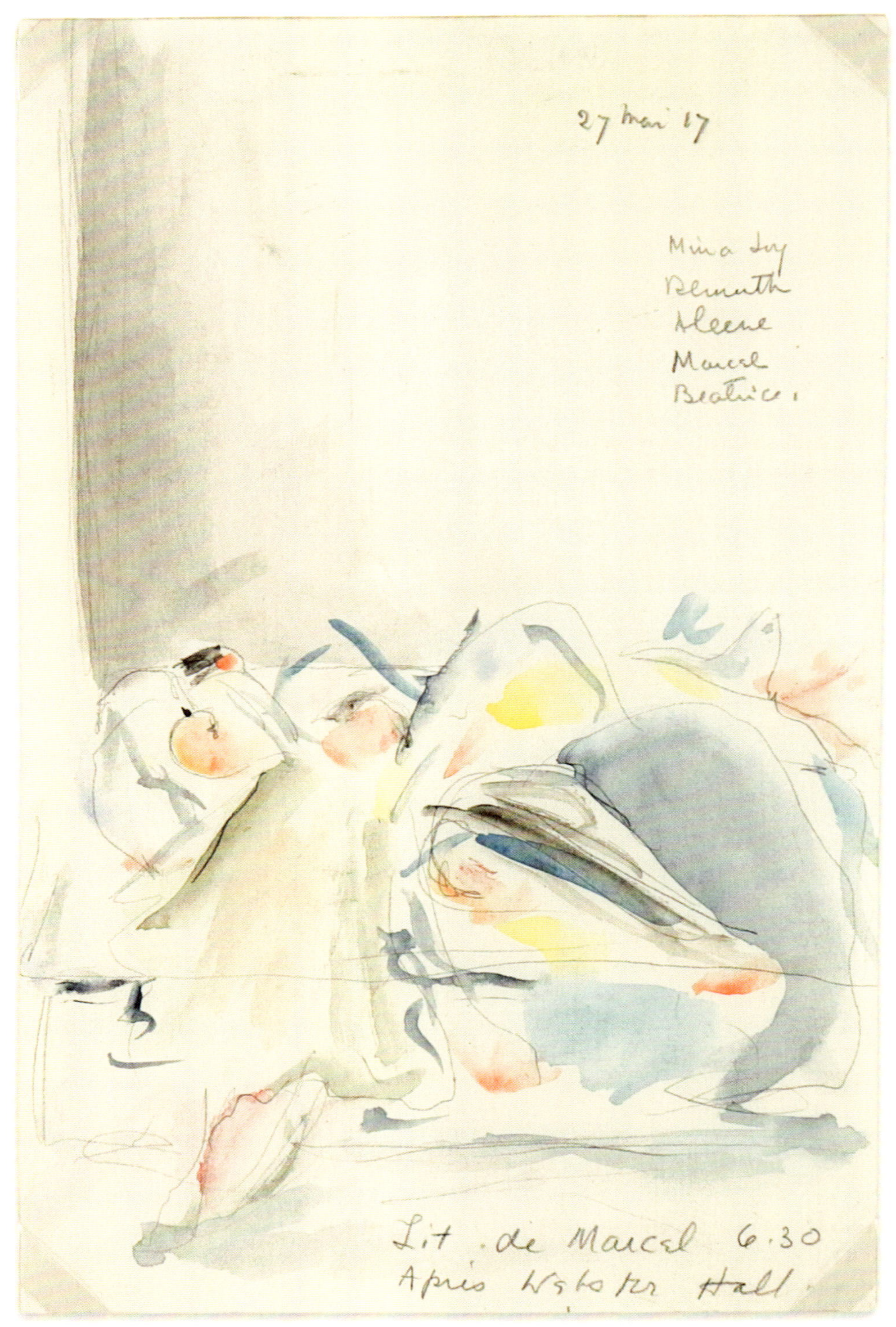

Beatrice Wood, *Lit de Marcel* (Marcel's Bed). Pencil and watercolor on paper 8⅛ x 5¼″
Collection of Francis M. Naumann and Marie T. Keller. Photograph by Dana Williams.

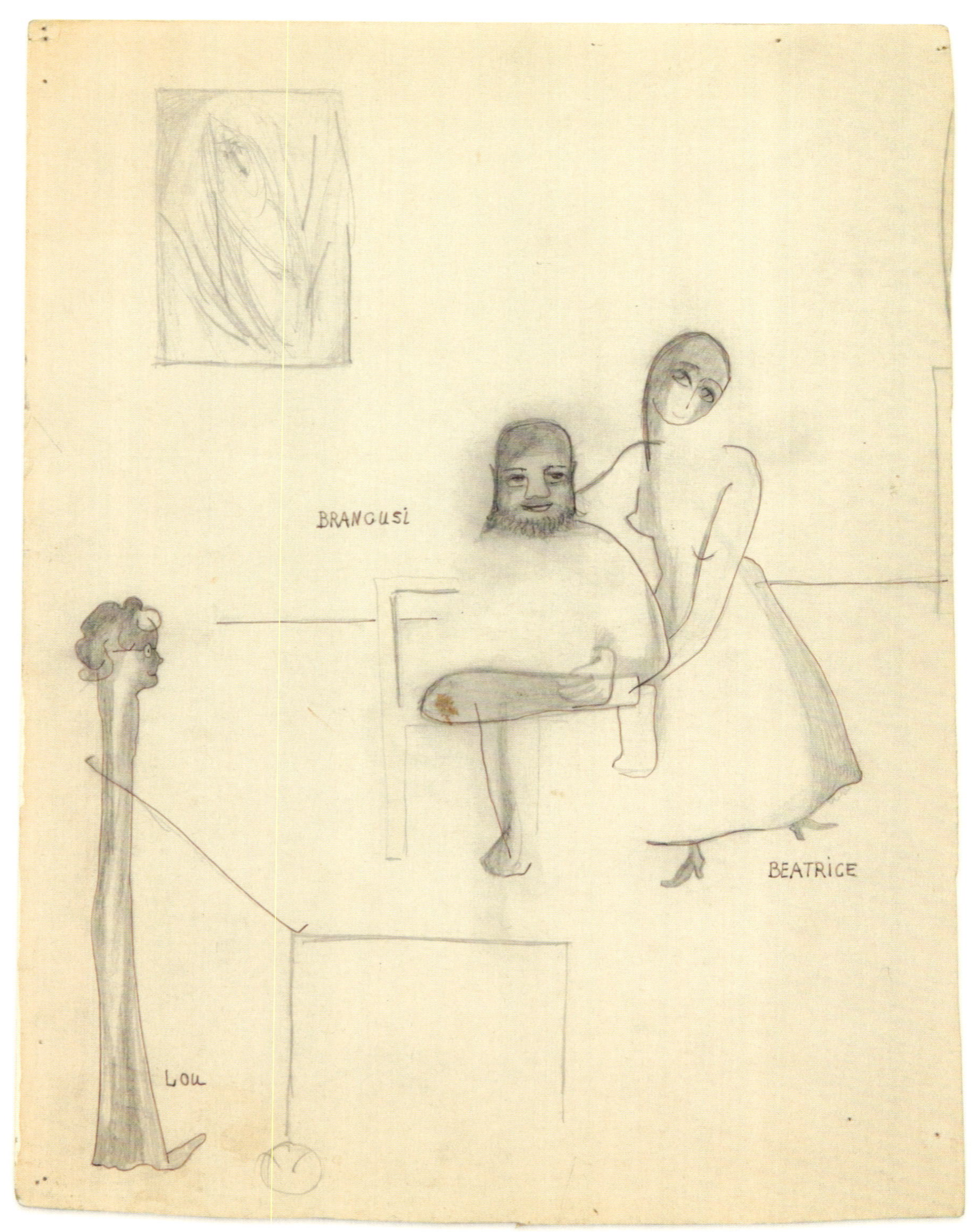

Untitled, Undated, Illustration on cardstock, 15 x 10¾"
"Brancusi, Beatrice, Lou."

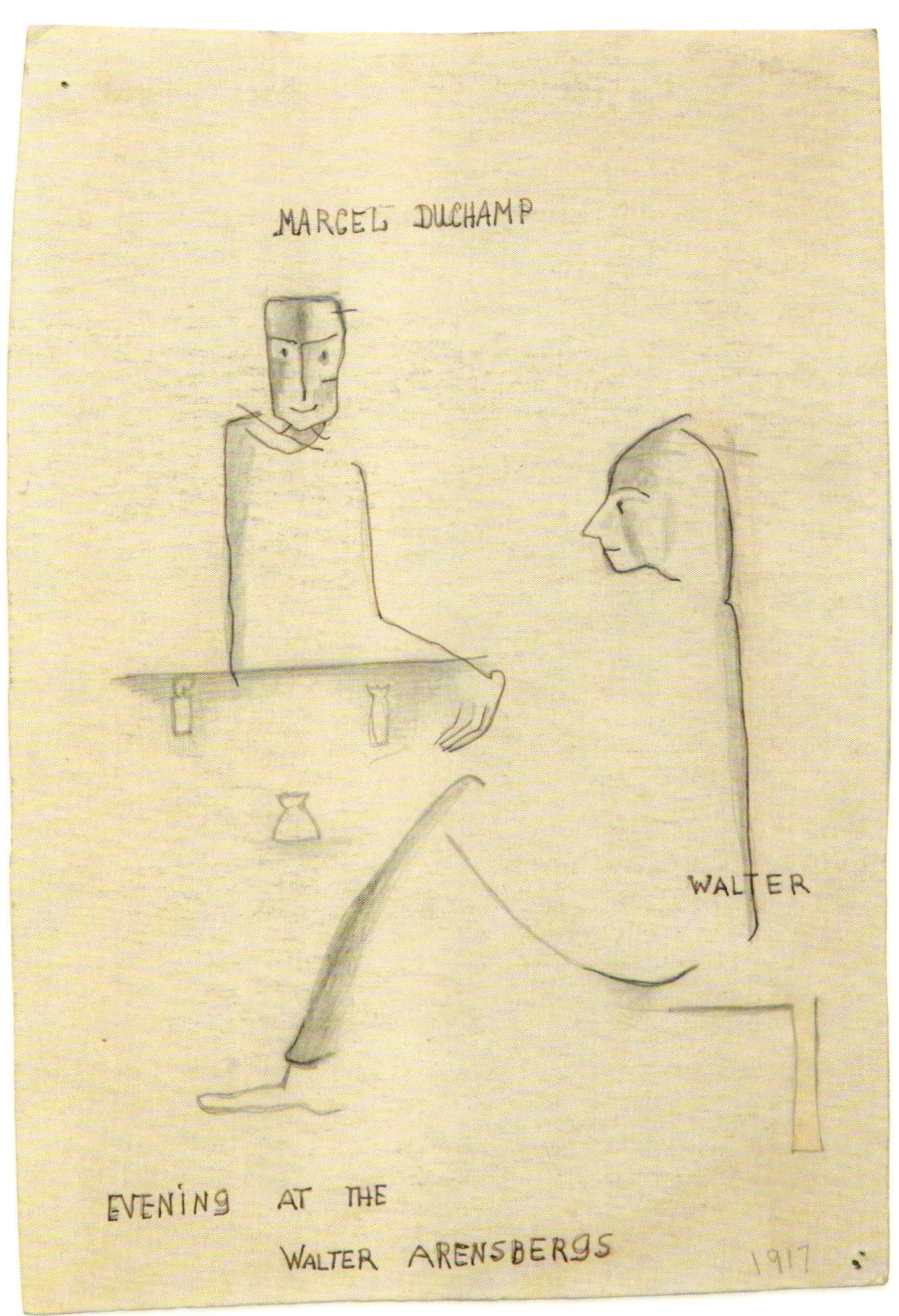

Evening at the Walter Arensbergs, Undated, Illustration on paper, 9¼ x 6¼"
"Marcel Duchamp, Walter"

memories or episodes inspired Roché, but the characters bear only passing resemblance to those of us in real life!

But Roché did write about the three of them in his unfinished novel, *Victor*.

There is disagreement among Dada scholars whether she and Duchamp were lovers. The latter is unlikely in the grander sense, but it is likely that they had a casual moment or two between the sheets. Duchamp was promiscuous and gave himself freely to any port in a storm.

I once asked Beato point blank, "What was Duchamp like in bed?" Her answer? "It was much like shaking hands. Sex for him was an impersonal act. True intimacy was friendship." And as proof of their deeper connection, they remained close for his entire life.

The Dada group organized an exhibition, *Independents Salon*, modeled after the the French *Société des Artistes Indépendents*, which allowed anyone to show a work for a fee, *sans* a jury. It was at this exhibition that Duchamp anonymously submitted his *Fountain*, an industrially-made *urinor* signed "R. Mutt." It is now the most famous ceramic and modern art object in the world.

The jury (which included Duchamp) reneged on its rules and refused entry to this work. Standing next to Beato at that moment, Duchamp without revealing his authorship resigned from the jury and walked out. A few weeks later Beato wrote in *Blindman* magazine that the decision was ridiculous. After all, "plumbing and bridges" were America's greatest aesthetic achievement.

Her painting of a nude woman with an actual bar of heart-shaped soap strategically attached, was accepted and became a secondary *success de scandale* due to an unintended error. She had meant to write, "*Un peu de savon dans l'eau*" (A little soap in some water) but in error wrote, "*Un Peat [sic] deau dans suovon*" (A little water in some soap). It seems innocent enough but was read as wildly provocative. She offered to change the title, but Duchamp insisted that she keep the libidinous label. Men, sensing a free spirit, festooned the painting with their calling cards. The critics, however, were less seduced, with one deriding it as "the keynote of childish whim." Beato cheerfully and fully agreed with the assessment.

She was now successfully introduced to New York culture, not as a debutante, but as a flower of the new avant-garde. In 1918 she takes to the stage, joining the French Repertory Theater in New York, playing over forty *ingénue* roles—a young, pretty, vulnerable, and innocent female lead or secondary lead. She also married a Belgian scoundrel to whom she unattractively referred as a "faded Mussolini."

Her parents were horrified and set a private detective on his tail, discovering that he was a bigamist with at least one other wife living in Brussels. The marriage had not been consummated and was quickly annulled. But the marriage served its purpose— now as a once-married woman, she could escape her mother's grip on her life.

Later she toured on the vaudeville circuit, and from this, recounts her first giving over to sex purely for lust. One of the performers was an acrobat whose act involved falling off tables. His muscled neck was so sexy that Beato spent a night with him. But the next morning "he ate his breakfast with a knife and he called me 'Cookie' and that was the end of that."

She says that the purpose of the fling was to gain bragging rights. "I slept with a man who falls off tables for a living." But the more important lesson she discovered was that there was no pleasure in sex that was purely physical. There had to be a strong romantic and emotional attachment.

This was hardly an impediment. Though she lists seven loves in her life, those are just the major ones. There were others, briefer, and less memorable. As she remarked, "If a man…. I would fall into his lap like overripe fruit."

PART TWO: AFTER DADA

1933. Beato is now 40 years old, her career in theater and vaudeville behind her. She is living in Los Angeles, enticed to join the Dada collectors Walter and Louise Arensberg in the City of Angels.

Once in Los Angeles she took on odd jobs and subsisted as best she could on a small monthly stipend from a rich aunt. This was fortunate because after her father died, her mother tore through the family wealth, mortgaged everything, leaving her daughter with one Railroad Bond worth $1,000 as her inheritance.

Why is 1933 key? That is the year Beato enrolled at the very stylish, newly completed Hollywood High School, taking an adult education class in ceramics. Her goal was to stay just long enough to make a teapot and some cups. A simple task, she thought.

She was trying to match her new creations to the French *rococo* luster plates that she had bought from an antique shop in Haarlem in the Netherlands three years earlier, while attending a meeting hosted by Krishnamurti, her spiritual guide. He would later locate to Ojai and would remain a central influence throughout her life.

After six weeks in class she realized that she lacked the skill to make a teapot (the most complex of vessels), but did manage to complete and fire two crudely formed plates and a pair of handbuilt figures. The latter were charmingly naïve and sold for $2.50 a piece. With these sales, she was unknowingly taking her first steps towards joining the nascent studio art pottery movement in Southern California. It would launch her international career that, remarkably, lasted for the next sixty-five years.

While her meager sales may seem inconsequential, Wood was living on "my miserable seventy-three dollars a month income." She figured that selling only three figures a month would increase her monthly allowance by over ten percent. Her primary goal she recalled "was economic, not artistic. The Depression was on."

Next came Steve Hoag. She met him at a dinner party where he was her blind date. Steve was not Beatrice's type, "too Yankee" for her taste. He was often morose, too conventional, asexual, and suffered from a common neuropsychiatric disorder, Tourette's Syndrome, that worsened as he aged.

However, Hoag was kind and became, despite her protests and lack of encouragement, a valued friend, financial advisor (goodness knows she needed one, not even able to balance a checkbook), and her defender, ensuring that her career progressed.

His friends were mostly of no interest to her, "too stuffy," except for one couple, Jack and Frances Case. In her autobiography she writes:

> I liked them the moment we met. They were up to date, liberal people in their forties. Jack had been an Olympic hurdler, traveled with the team to Russia, and met Frances in Paris. They lived together for two years and then decided to marry "for the convenience, the trap of all who love."

Jack was a successful advertising man. He and Frances had a lease on a 20-acre property on nearby Del Mar. They would invite friends to join them for a weekend of *life au naturel* at the adjoining deserted beach. No one paid any attention, except for those on the passing trains of the Southern Pacific Railroad.

I, however, the liberal one, having seen nude models since I was sixteen years old studying art at the Julian Academy in Paris, could not get myself into the ocean without a swimsuit. Even Steve did not hesitate to plunge in naked.

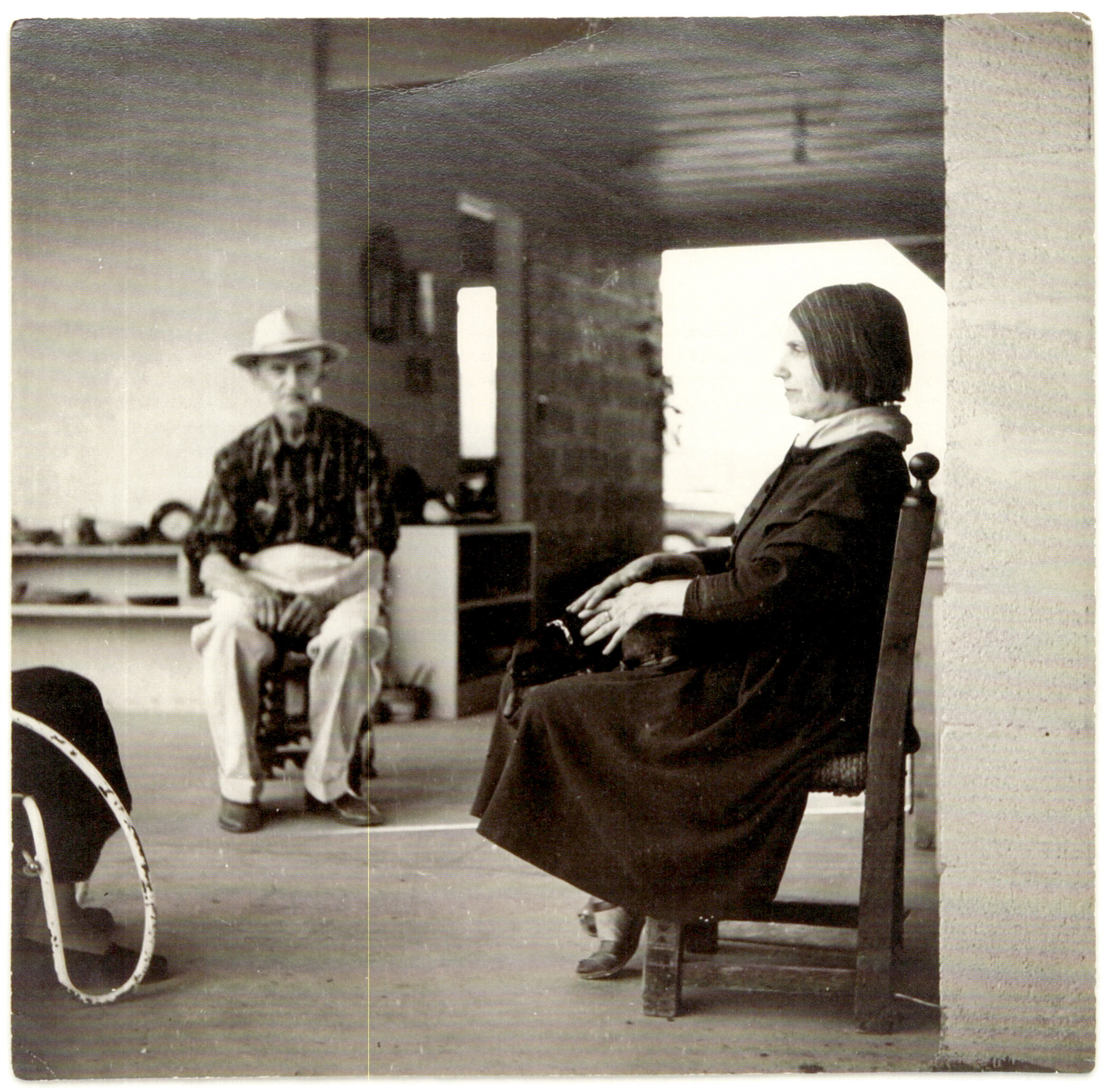

Jack Case, *"Ojai Gothic (Beato and Steve),"* 1953-54. 10½ x 10⅜"

She blames her shyness on her mother's stern moral admonitions, but soon outgrew her reserve. And then some. Shortly after she and Jack met, they began (with the permission of Frances—Jack believed in open relationships) to have sex. An illustrated letter dated 1939 gives a sense of their good-natured relationship.

"Jack, my dear, dearest: When I first met you my legs were together. Like this." (Sketches in the letter graphically illustrate "open" and "closed.") "Desire had not touched me, sin as the world calls the cosmic urge I felt for you, had passed me by. With you came the transformation... the strong hands of those who sin, but tell not." Beatrice

Steve was not part of her romantic life. Yet he recognized that she needed some stability, security, and a studio, if her career were to grow. He encouraged her to buy a property in what is now North Hollywood and build a duplex with him as the anchor tenant. He and Jack designed her studio. She opened a shop at the Legendary Crossroads of the World in Hollywood and her career began, if not to boom, at least to grow.

In February of 1938 a massive storm hit Los Angeles. It poured for two weeks at the end of which Beato had lost not just her house and every possession, but even the land was swept away. And that was how she was married for the second time.

Steve convinced her that the Red Cross would not give financial aid to a single woman and so they married. Whether for that reason or not, she received $500 which enabled her to build a new home and studio. Always with a soft spot for strays and loyal to a fault, Beato allowed Steve to continue to live with her for the rest of his life.

Neither marriage was consummated. Beato admitted to having fallen in love seven times, but never married a man she loved. It was just as well, as some turned out to be less than ideal part-ner material. "I do not know" she later said, "whether that makes me a good girl gone bad, or a bad girl gone good."

By the time Beato moved to Ojai in 1948, much had changed. Although Steve still lived with her, his Tourette's was growing worse. He would storm through the studio while she was selling her work to wealthy ladies from Beverly Hills, letting forth a tor-rent of foul language. Unfazed, Beato would turn to the startled women, frozen in horror, and airily say, "Good help is so difficult to find, don't you think?"

Her career had taken a dramatic turn. She had moved from entrepreneur to artist after studying with the great ceramic artist Glenn Lukens and an equally talented couple, Gertrud and Otto Natzler, who in 1939 had relocated from Vienna to Los Angeles, fleeing the Third Reich. It was no longer enough to make a few *bibelots* each month. She wanted to excel in ceramics—she wanted to create masterpieces, and she did.

Beato never lost that moment of wonderment when she spotted those luster plates in Holland in 1930. Their surfaces followed and haunted her like a glistening hummingbird. Step by step, error by error, and with some expert help along the way, she mastered the elusive art of luster glazing with metallic shimmer and magical iridescence. Beato achieved this in her own funky and informal manner with a somewhat reckless disregard for craft rules, preferring risk to order.

The luster glazes struck a chord with the public and her career surged with many solo exhibitions. This included the Honolulu Academy of Arts in 1951, a one person show, *Ceramics of Beatrice Wood* at America House in New York in 1955 (with the cover design of her exhibition catalog by Duchamp), *Ceramics: Beatrice Wood,* at the Pasadena Art Museum 1959, Takashimaya Department Store in Tokyo (the most prestigious venue for potters in Japan) in 1962. In 1964-65 *Beatrice Wood an Exhibition* travelled from the California Legion of Honor in San Francisco to the Santa Barbara Museum of Art. This exhibition produced one of the finest of her many reviews, written by Anaïs Nin, famous for her published journals and as the first major woman author to write erotica. A good fit.

Nin, writing for *Artforum,* commented:

> People sometimes look wistfully at pieces of ancient ceramics in museums as if such beauty were part of a lost and buried past. But Beatrice Wood is a modern ceramist creating objects today that would enhance your life. The colors, textures and forms are at once vivid and subtle. The decorative ability is extended into portrayals of humor, euphoria, or contemplation. Her colors are molded with light. Some have tiny craters, as if formed

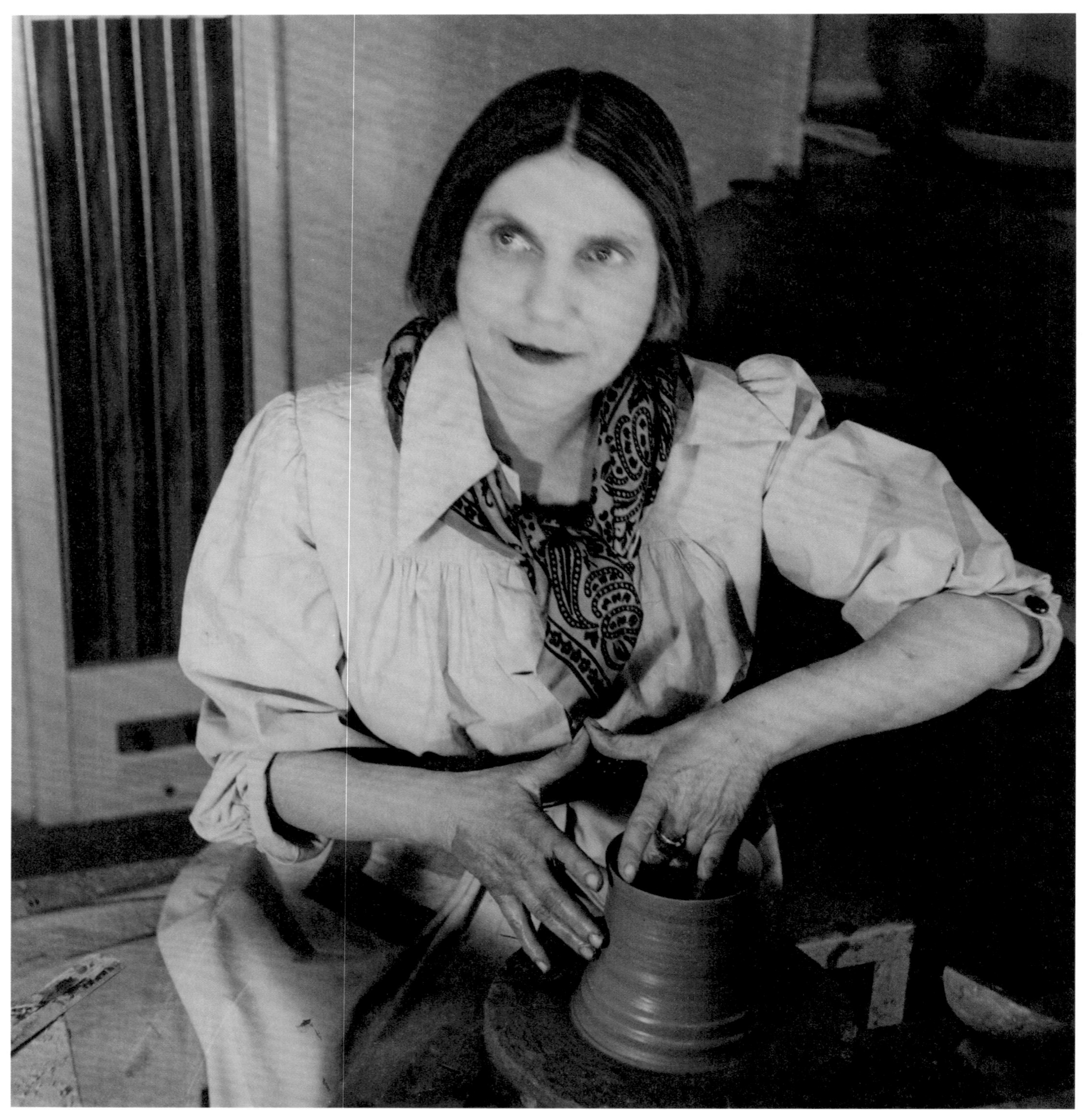

Jack Case, *Untitled* c. 1959, Silver Gelatin Print, from a scrapbook about Beatrice Wood compiled by and in the collection of Rhea and Jack Case. It is captioned: The artist is giving the base its first shape.

by the evolutions, contractions, and expansions of the earth itself. Some seem made of shells or pearls, others are iridescent and smoky like trailways left by satellites.

Jack was still in her life. Frances had died, and Jack lived in Ojai. He was no longer an advertising man, having taken up photography. Then in 1950 he became the producer of *Cavalcade of Books*, a highly popular TV show that ran for twenty years. In 1953 he received the Peabody Award for the best educational show in America alongside Bennett Cerf, Edward R. Murrow, and Chet Huntley. The Peabody citation for the award explains its value:

> The Peabody Awards Committee dismisses as piffle the theory that, because of television, fewer good books are being read in America. There is no substitute for really good books. Television, as a matter of fact, can materially help to spread the word about the joys of reading, and *Cavalcade of Books* is an excellent example of just how this can be accomplished. Produced by expert showmen, backed solidly by the book-selling fraternity of California and the leading publishers of America, *Cavalcade of Books* on KNXT is now being watched by upward of 350,000 people a week. The Peabody Committee (three of whose members know from personal participation the pulling power of the program) hopes that this award may stimulate bookmen in other parts of the country to similar endeavor. Under the heading of television education, therefore, we present the George Foster Peabody Award to *Cavalcade of Books*.

Some years ago, a treasure came up on auction—the hardcover television station guest registry for *Cavalcade of Books*, signed by approximately 840 celebrities, authors, and artists, some on affixed slips, with the signatures dating from October 28, 1956 up to March 22, 1970. Each guest had signed in, with many adding additional information or inscriptions, including the date, addresses, or book title under their signature. Others had signed multiple times, including some of the more interesting ones: Charles Schulz, Dr. Seuss, Ray Bradbury, Eddie Cantor, Irving Stone, Art Linkletter, Edith Head, Harold Lloyd, Buster Keaton, Aldous Huxley, Langston Hughes, Groucho Marx, Meredith Wilson, Vincent Price, Hal Holbrook, Roy Rogers, Dale Evans, Zsa Zsa Gabor, William Peter Blatty, Julia Child, Polly Bergen, Christopher Isherwood, Jean Renoir, Sessue Hayakawa, Will and Ariel Durant, Inger Stevens, Pauline Kael, Mel Blanc, Jacqueline Susann, Irving Wallace, Mel Torme, and Sid Fleischman… and Beatrice Wood.

In 1956 Beato's casual affair with Jack was tested. He decided to marry Rhea who was his host on the TV show. Hearing of their marriage, Beato sent a provocative but funny letter to Rhea. In the papers at the American Archive of Art in Washington DC, Rhea left a card attached to the letter explaining her first exposure to Beato:

> By way of explanation about this letter—I had met Steve through Jack. Steve took me to Ojai—while Beato was in Portugal—I had not yet met Beato. I returned to NYC and Steve told Beato about my visit to Ojai and meeting Jack and all.
>
> When I returned to NYC I received this note from Beato— a real sorta shock—who was this person??? A week later Jack came to NYC and all of the sudden we were married (on top of the tombs down in Wall St. by the big Judge Sweickert). After I married, Jack came back to Calif.— he took me to Ojai to meet this Beato and what an experience!!!! Her wedding cards to us—carry on this "left-tit motif."

Beato's letter, dated October 3, 1956 was no doubt startling to a newlywed and reads as follows, minus a few edits about her daily life. "Dear Rhea: Though you are 36 on my list of 54 letters to be written, I am cheating, passing you up to 15, as I just cannot let that Jack Case get to New York without telling you my left tit belongs to him, and his left ……. Hoping you will be coming West soon, so that I can cut your throat." Beatrice

She and Rhea became friends the moment they met and Rhea, a hugely accomplished student of literature and media star, remained in awe of Beato for her entire life. Rhea, for her part, took on responsibility for growing and guiding Beato's intellectual pursuits and the maintenance of her health. After she and Jack moved to Los Angeles, Rhea supplied Beato with books and insisted on a regime of vitamins and herbal supplements, which she custom packaged and mailed to Beato with instructions as to their use and benefits.

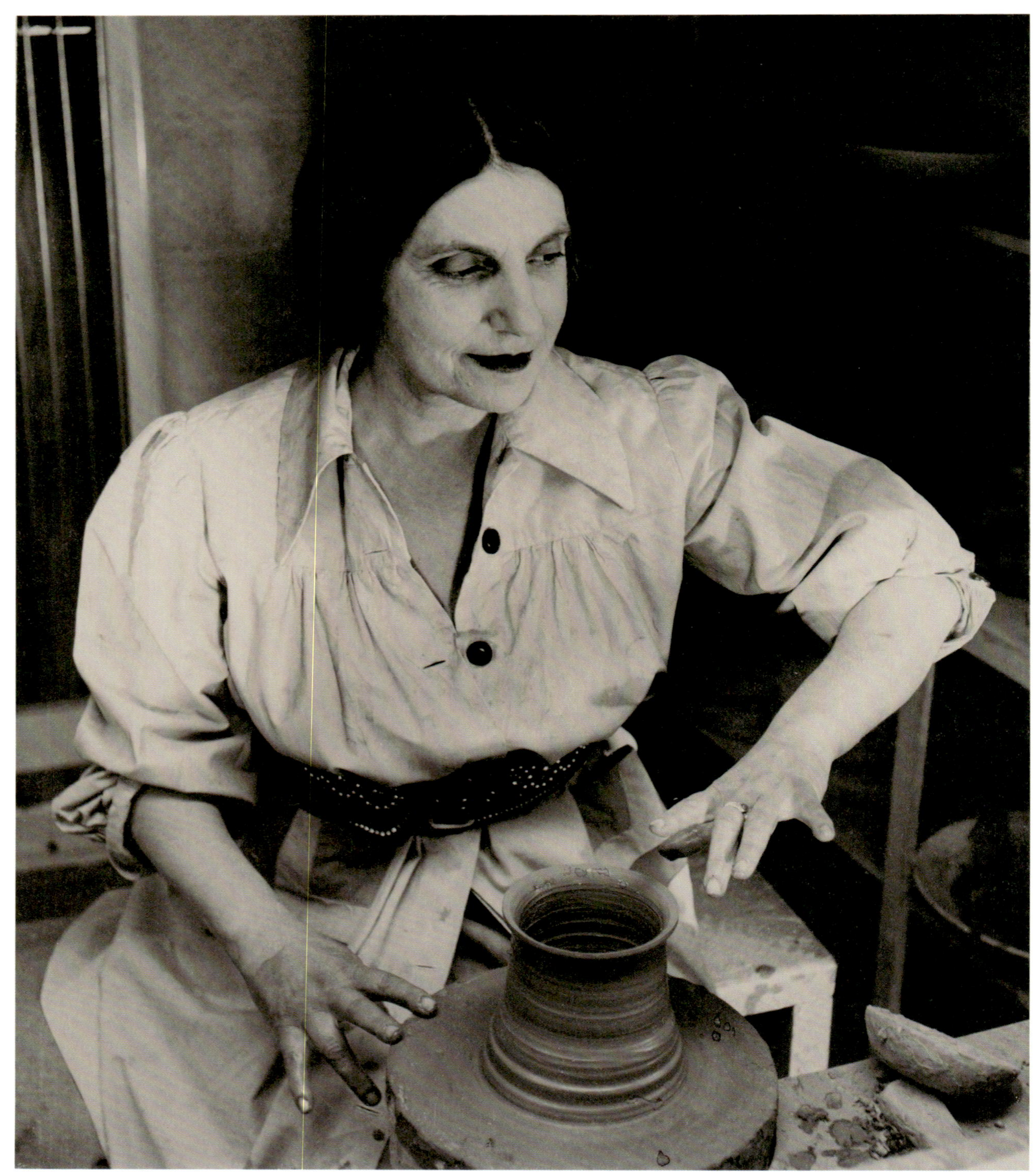

Jack Case, *Untitled* c. 1959, Silver Gelatin Print, from a scrapbook about Beatrice Wood compiled by and in the collection of Rhea and Jack Case. It is captioned: The artist is beginning to wide (sic) the top of the vase.

There is no record of the process by which the three negotiated their friendship and became occasional lovers. There is also no indication in any correspondence that this caused the slightest problem in the marriage or any jealousy. My guess is that the magic was humor, a quality all three were blessed with in abundance, as well as simply not taking their playful intimacy seriously.

Their liaison was emotional, perhaps based in a love of art and literature, and sex was the occasional *frisson*. I have not come across nor made an effort to dig up any personal details about their *ménage à trois* other than it existed. It is the overall spirit of their mutual love that is the glow in this book, not the details. Beato, however, to her credit, sometimes does leave little to the imagination in her drawings, all the way down to her hairy legs and pubic hair meticulously detailed in cotton.

The letters below, filled with details of her everyday life, communicate the growing warmth between Beato and Rhea and the irony that Jack became almost secondary in their relationship. The letters were most chaste with occasional reminders of their special relationship,

On November 5, 1959 Beato writes to Rhea with a final paragraph, "It is perfectly agreeable for Jack only to send me hugs by letter. The other chapter of our friendship will be taken care of when I see him in person."

In another letter on November 5, 1961 written at the American Embassy, New Delhi, India, where she was on a cultural exchange program for the State Department, Beato thanks Rhea for an unusual travel gift:

> Dear Rhea,
> The trip is simply fabulous. Such beauty and sights as I have seen. Bangkok a dream. New Delhi, a beautiful city of large spaces.
>
> Thank Jack for two things, telling me to keep a diary, which I write up daily, and letting myself be an important person. I have to think about it and remember. For certainly I am being threatened as me. I just pinch myself and make my self accept it. They have given me a car and a chauffeur, so that all day I can rush through the many appointments.

And thank you for letting Jack's feet be around me at night! For I would perish without their warmth to put me to sleep. I have always said a man's feet were better than a hot water bottle. I am cold at night, have no electric blanket. I put two coats in the bed, and then the good, comforting Jack-socks. Beato

In 1970 *Cavalcade of Books* comes to an end and the Cases move to San Diego, which Beato says is too far to travel and too costly to phone. Often there is a plaintiff quality in her letters as she asks time and again, "Are you happy having moved so far away from me?"

The letters continue with those between the two women growing ever more caring and loving. As always there was the flirtation from Beato with Jack with Rhea being the go-between. One May 31, 1972, she writes. "There seems to be a rascal down your way who wants drawings that he should not look at. Into the meat grinder with him. He better be careful, or he might get a drawing that even he would prefer not to look at."

One of the last letters in the Case's papers dated October 5, 1975 is after Jack's death. Rhea writes:

> My Dear Beato:
> Another beautiful letter from you. I save them all carefully. They mean so much to me. They are full of the wisdom that comes from quiet contemplation. You are putting so many things in order in your wonderful mind. I miss visiting with you. I am glad that you approve of my class in Meditation. The teacher and I have struck up a fine friendship. We are both Aquarians and so enjoy visiting with each other. She is very unassuming in nature—has so much to give to others You would so like her. She lectures all over the world, etc.
>
> You mention that often you think of Jack when you draw. I so often think of you and the fun you made for him with your drawings. I do believe that you must draw some more— because of the dream I had about you—that I must urge you to draw, and also—Jack was going to be an illustrator until he found out that he was color blind. He would love to help you in your drawing. Please draw with his help. He would be there to help you do even better than ever. He would love to express himself thru you. I must come up

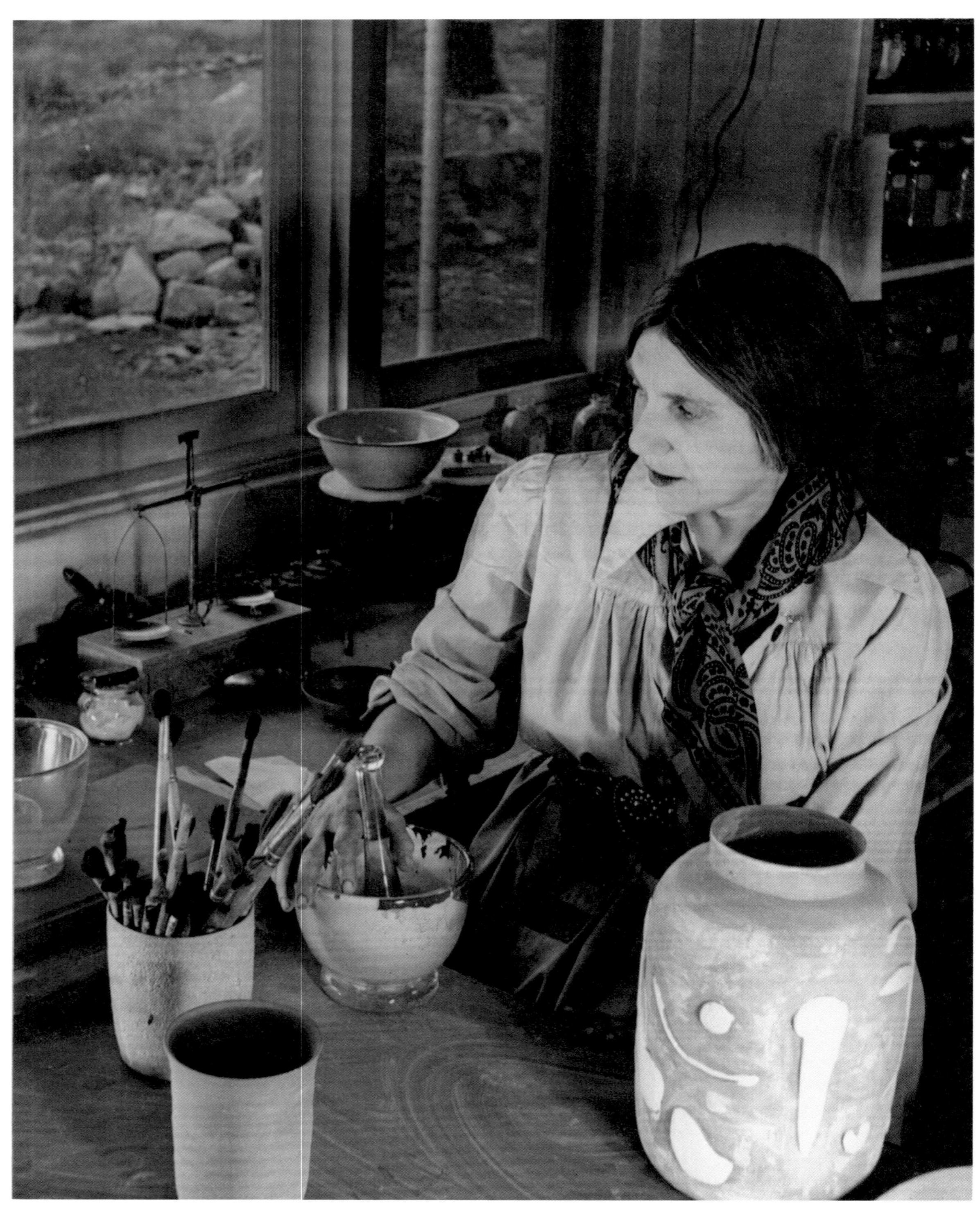

Jack Case, *Untitled* c. 1959, Silver Gelatin Print, from a scrapbook about Beatrice Wood
compiled by and in the collection of Rhea and Jack Case. It is captioned:
The artist preparing glaze which is needed to give the vase its finish.

later on this fall and see your new pottery. I treasure each piece I have of yours.

> I am back to work—taking care of Mrs. Dulin—Tues through Thursday—on that huge ranch. I was there doing this before Jack passed over. She is quite confused in her mind now—but pleads with me to stay with her. It is quite difficult—the confusion of her mind—when mine is so open.

Beatrice moved on, and communication with Rhea became rare. Jack passed in 1979 and Rhea outlived Beato, dying in 2005. There was no rupture in the friendship, just a gradual fade. Also, in part it was because in 1981 Beato began the most demanding, productive, and exciting halycon period of her career, and time for anything but her career was in short supply. In 1981 Mark Del Vecchio and I opened the Garth Clark Gallery in Los Angeles opposite the Los Angeles County Museum. It was the direct result of a visit with Beato in Ojai where she bemoaned that her life as an artist had amounted to nothing. She had not made a sale in years. Initially, we sold her work privately, but those months were awkward, and we did not enjoy selling in our home. Driving down Wilshire Boulevard one day I saw a "for rent" sign, and in September we opened with a sell-out show, *Beatrice Wood: A Very Private View*.

Beato was 87 years old when we started working with her and that relationship and treasured friendship continued until her death at 105. We organized from two to four exhibitions for her every year in our Los Angeles, New York, and Kansas City spaces as well as at museums here and abroad. She began to pile up honors and awards. Museums on five continents collected her work. She spoke at art symposiums and had two major national traveling retrospective exhibitions.

Now you may think this was exploitative, working an older artist so hard, but that was her lifeblood. When we were preparing for her second exhibition at the gallery, I would get calls from Beato about poor clay, misbehaving glazes, and a stubborn kiln with a mind of its own. Not knowing then about men being Mars and women being Venus, I assumed that the strain was too much and offered a solution. "Beatrice," I said, "We have a lot of your work in stock at the moment. You do not have to make new ceramics for the exhibition." She was silent for moment, then replied, firmly but not unkindly, "Do not ever say that to me again."

She never lost her seductive, sexual edge even though as the 1980s gave way to 1990s, it was just for the theatre, to exercise her wit, and to shock, which she adored doing. She was the eternal *ingénue* again, projecting her allure across the footlights, except that now her stages were art galleries and museums, and the spotlights were on her art.

Mark and I last visited her when she was 104 and a half. Six months later, a few days after her 105th birthday, she did what she always told me she could do at any time. She let go. But during our final visit she was in fine fettle, noting that it was a great pity that we had not arrived a few hours earlier. "This couple came to visit and brought their son. I have no idea how old he was. Fifteen, sixteen? But that did not matter because he was a gem of manhood. If I was three months younger, I would have gone for him.

Selected Bibliography

Garth Clark, *Gilded Vessel, The Lustrous Art and Life and Beatrice Wood*, Madison: Guild Publishing, 2001.
Beatrice Wood, *I Shock Myself*, Ojai: Dillingham Press (later republished by Chronical Press,) 1985.
——, *Touching Certain Things*, Los Angeles, MGM Press, 1992.
——, *Pinching Spaniards*, Ojai: Topa Topa, 1988.
——, *The Angel Who Wore Black Tights*, Ojai: Rogue Press, 1982.
——, *33rd Wife of a Maharajah: A Love Affair in India*, Bombay: Allied Publishers, 1992.
——, *Madam Lola's Pleasure Palace (as Countess Lola Screwinsky)*, Ojai: Beatrice Wood, 1994.
Beatrice Wood and Marlene Wallace, *Playing Chess with the Heart*, Chronicle Books, San Francisco, 1994.
Elsa Longhauser and Lisa Melandri, *Beatrice Wood: Career Woman—Drawings, Paintings, Vessels and Objects*, Santa Monica Museum of Art, Published with the Getty Foundation, 2012.
Francis M. Naumann, *New York Dada 1915-1923*, New York: Abrams, 1994.
Francis M. Naumann, Ed., *Beatrice Wood: A Centennial Tribute*, New York: American Craft Museum, 1997.
Henri Pierre Roché, "Victor" in Vol. 4, Jean Clair, *Marcel Duchamp Catalog Raisonné*, Paris: Centre National d'Art et de Culture, Georges Pompidou, 1977.

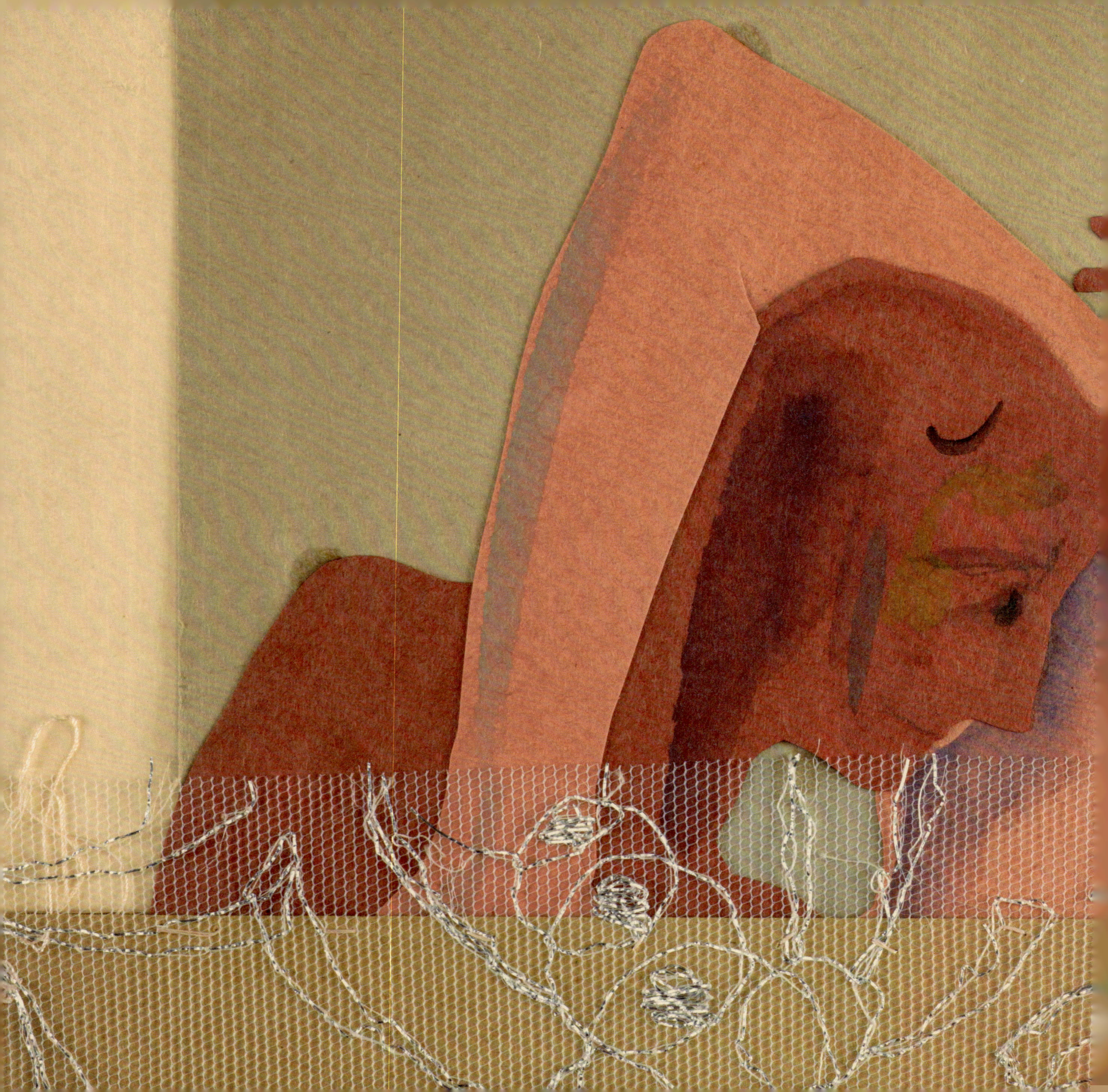

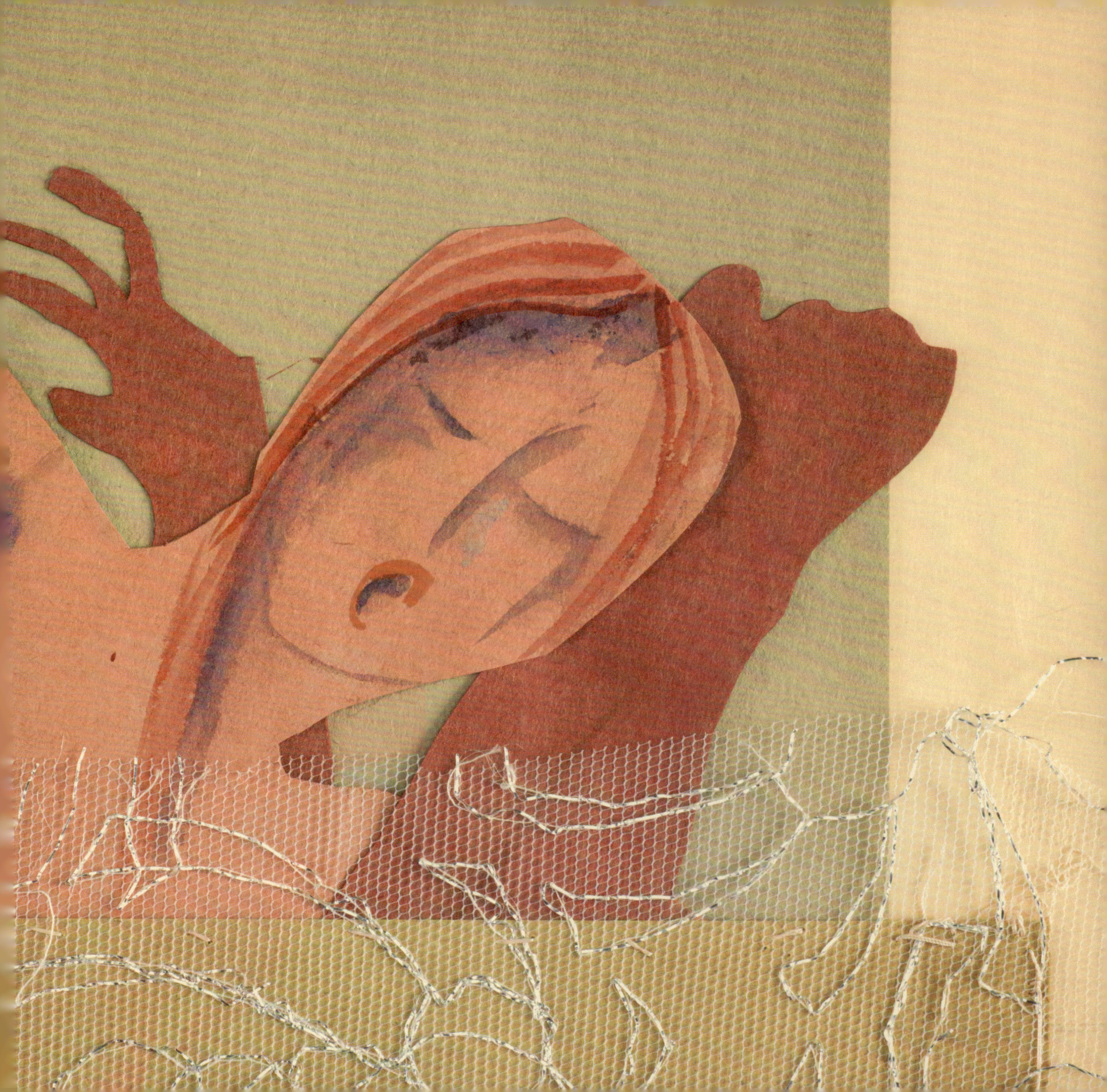

"A few days late...

But is That Not better than Two monThs..."

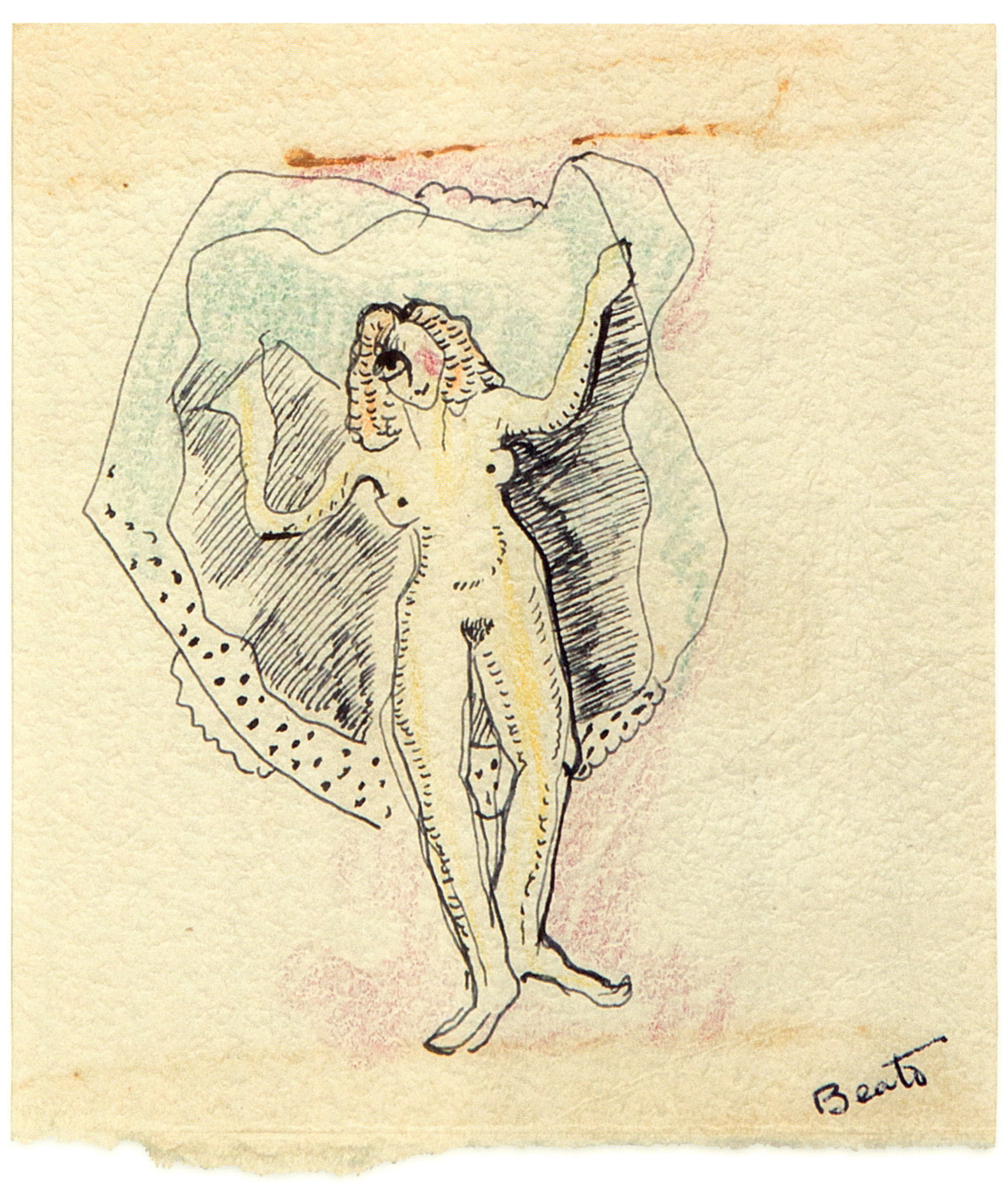

Untitled (4-page booklet), 1934, Illustration on paper, 6¼ x 5½" (folded), 6¼ x 10¼" (unfolded)

"To Special Special Jack."

"Love from three little pussies."

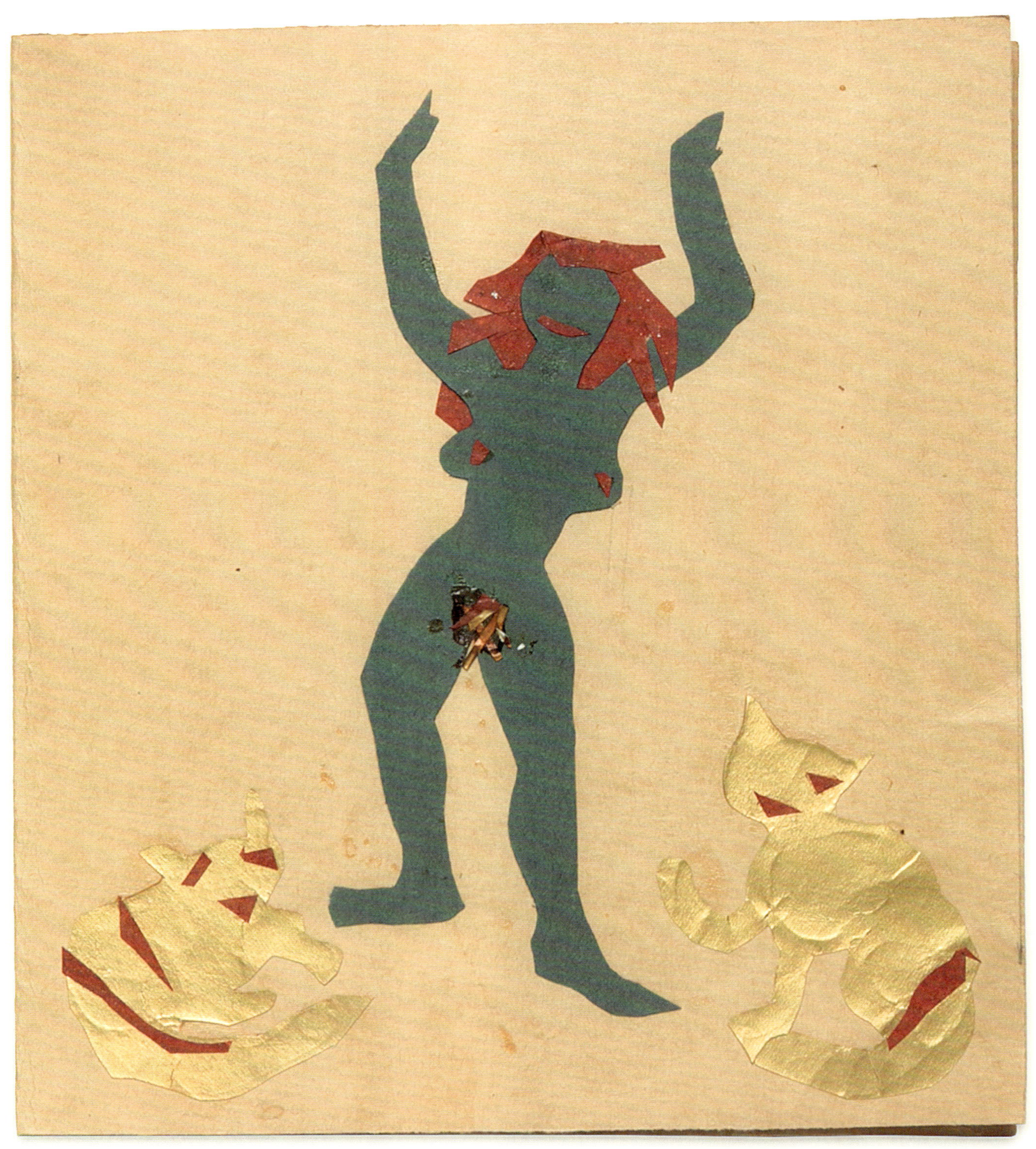

Untitled (4-page booklet), 1945, Paper collage, 6 x 6¾″ (folded), 6 x 13″ (unfolded)

Passion of Midnight

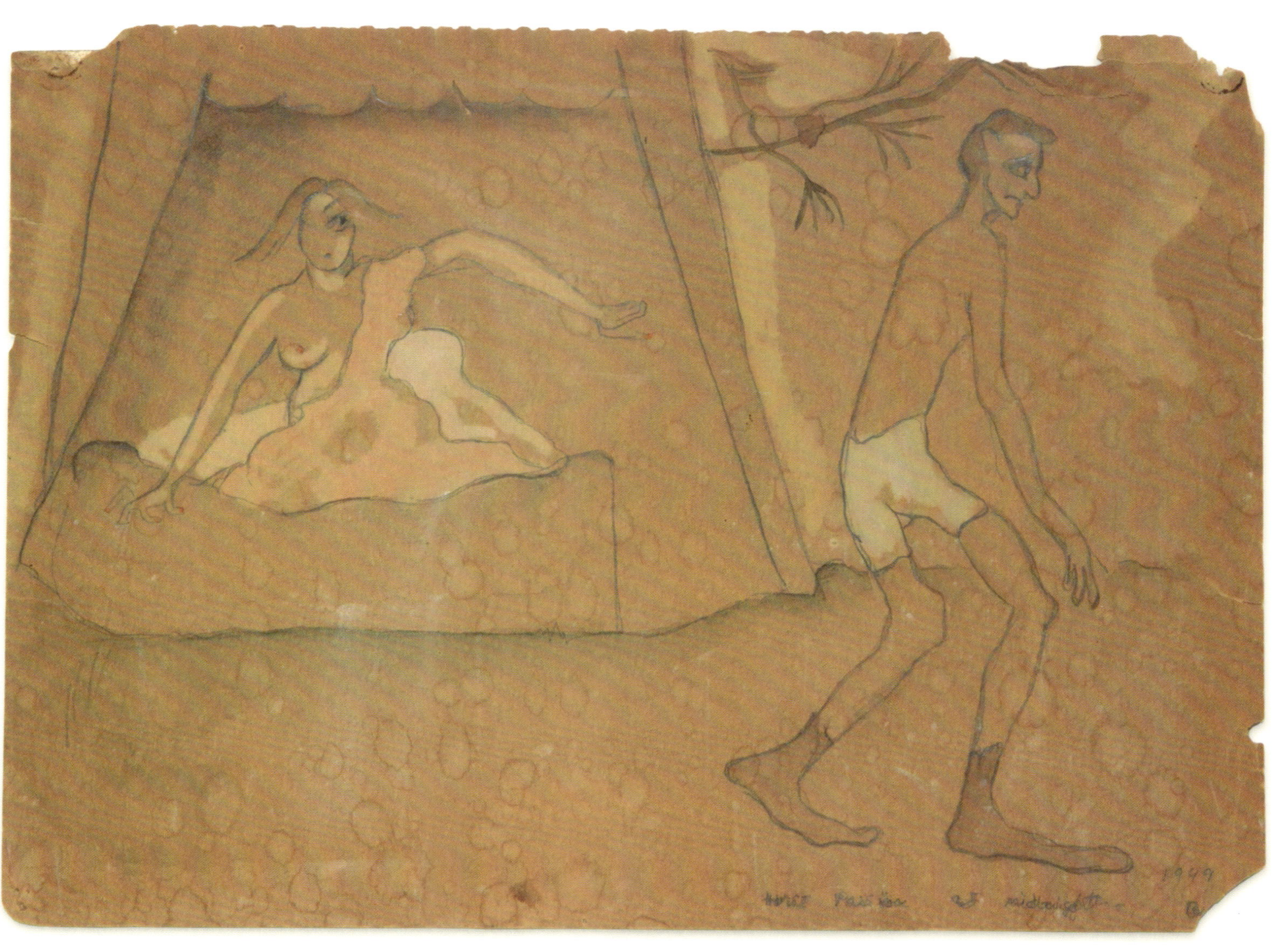

Passion of Midnight, 1949, Illustration on paper, 9½ x 12½″

"I set himself to examine the member."

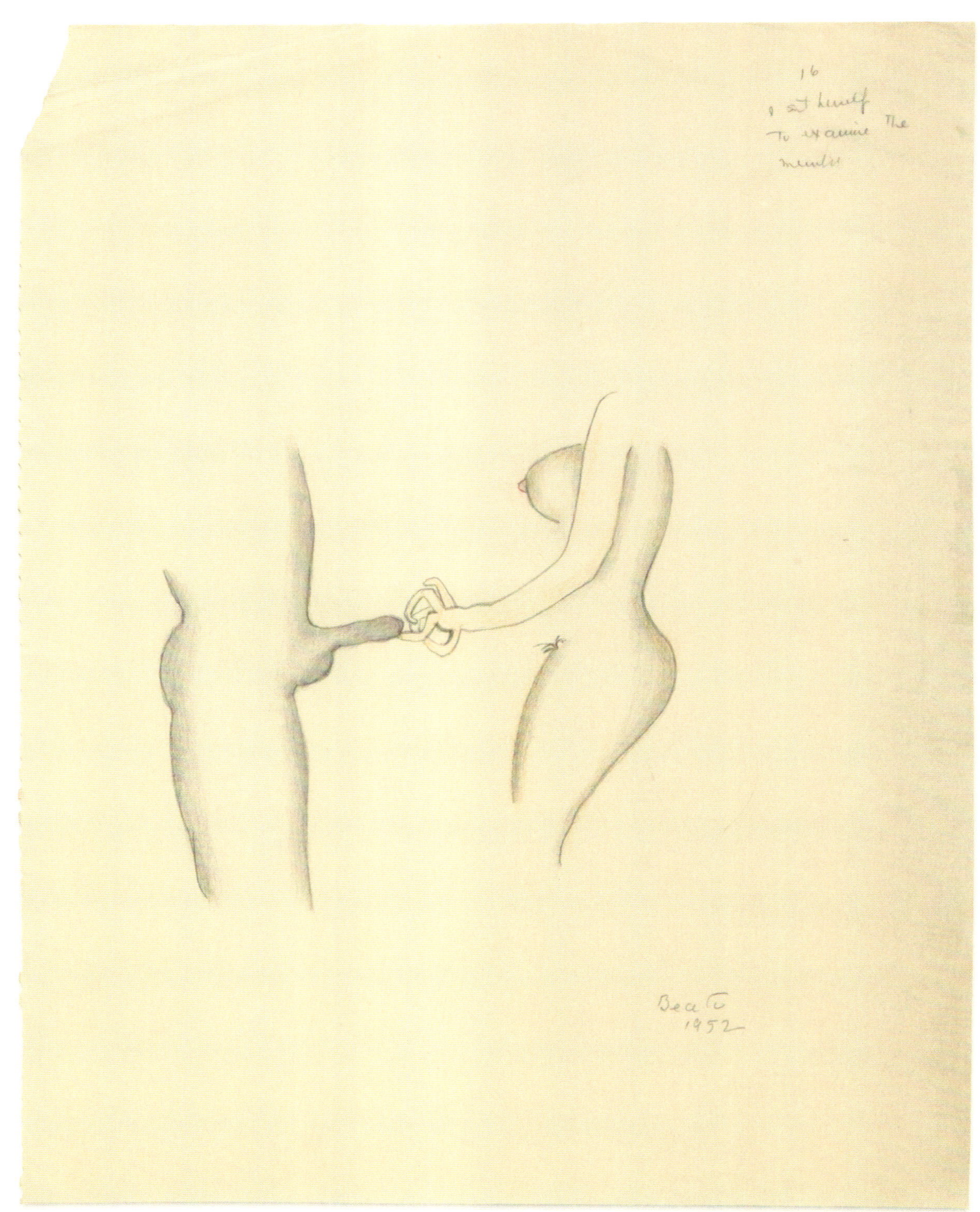

Untitled, 1952, Work on paper, 13 x 9"

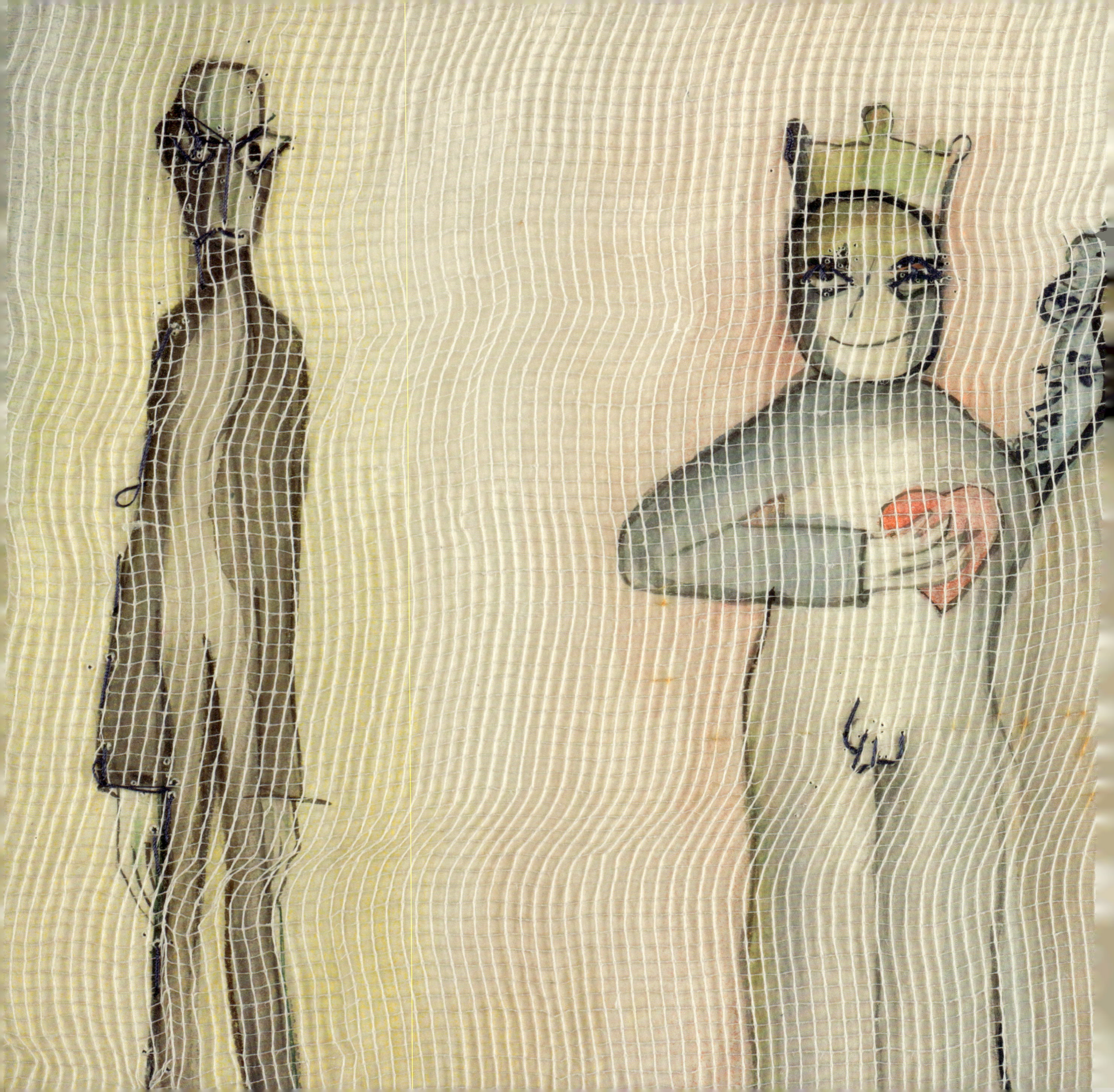

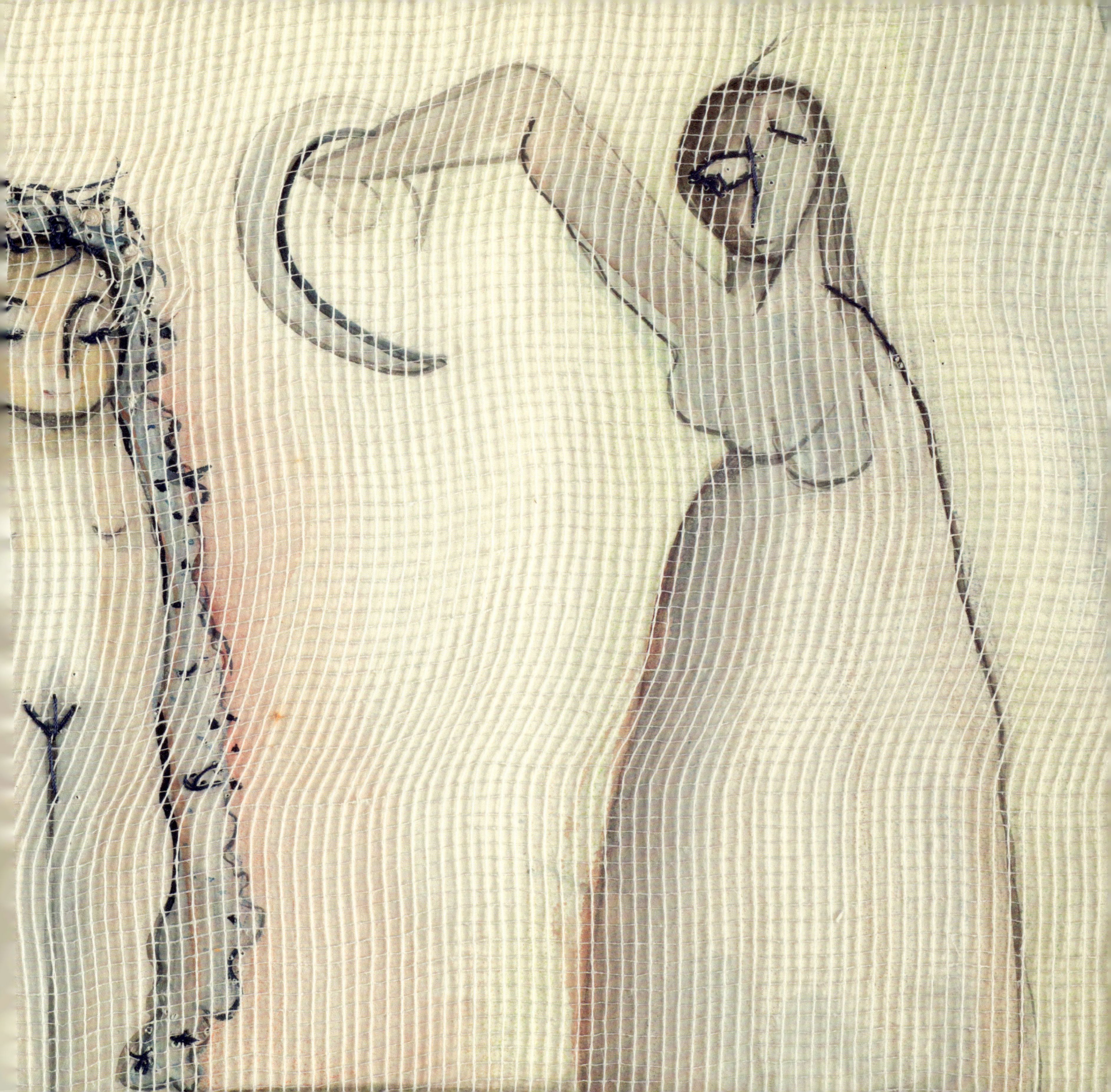

THE CUT-THROAT WEDDING of Jack AND RHEA CASE

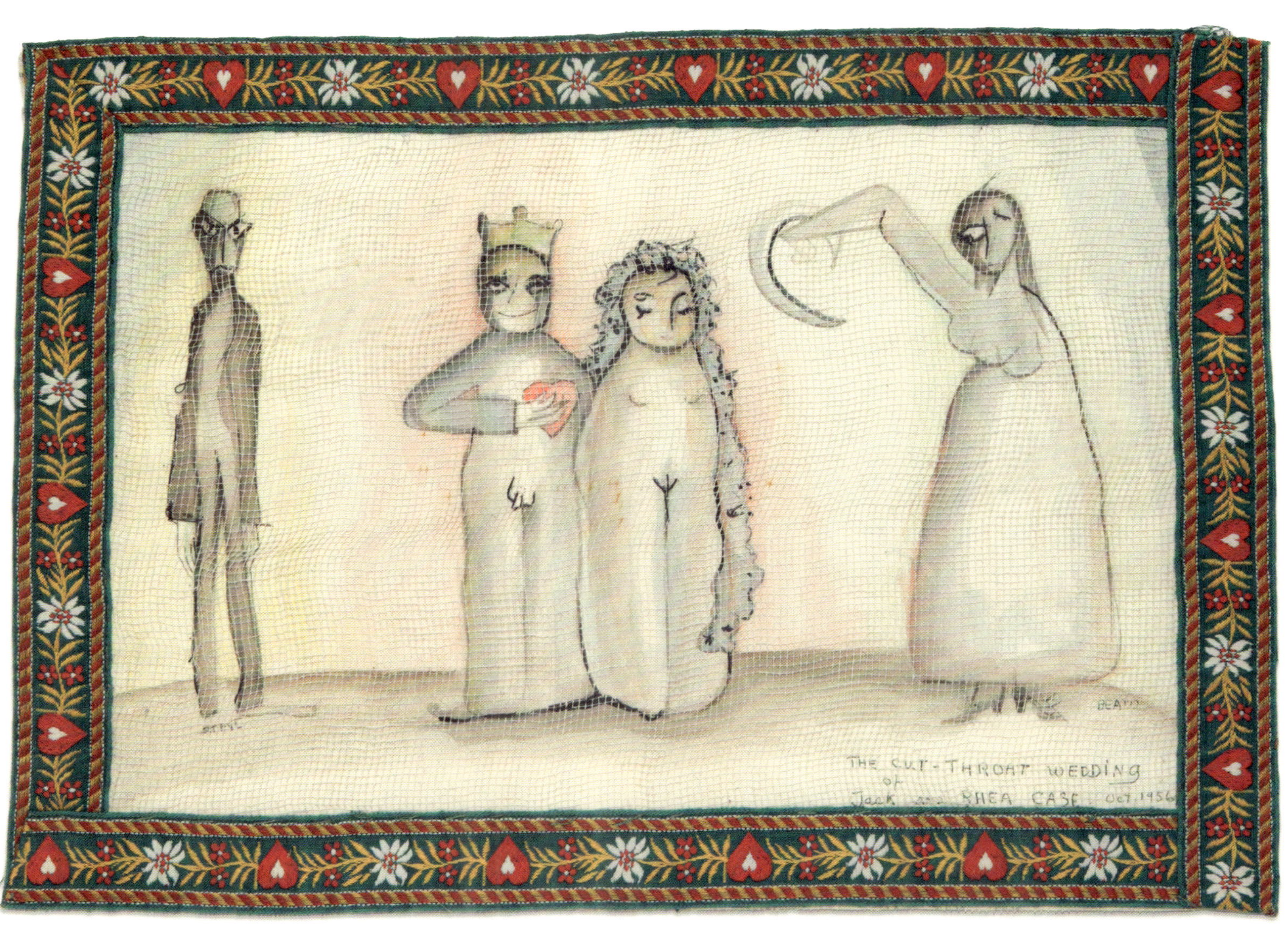

THE CUT-THROAT WEDDING of Jack AND RHEA CASE—Oct. 1956, 1956, Paper and fabric collage, 11 x 15½"

"*give HER AN ELECTRiC BLANKET for CHRiSTMAS—1956*"

"Steve says, '*I'll BE g—D!*
I'll don't like THAT kind of stuff.'"

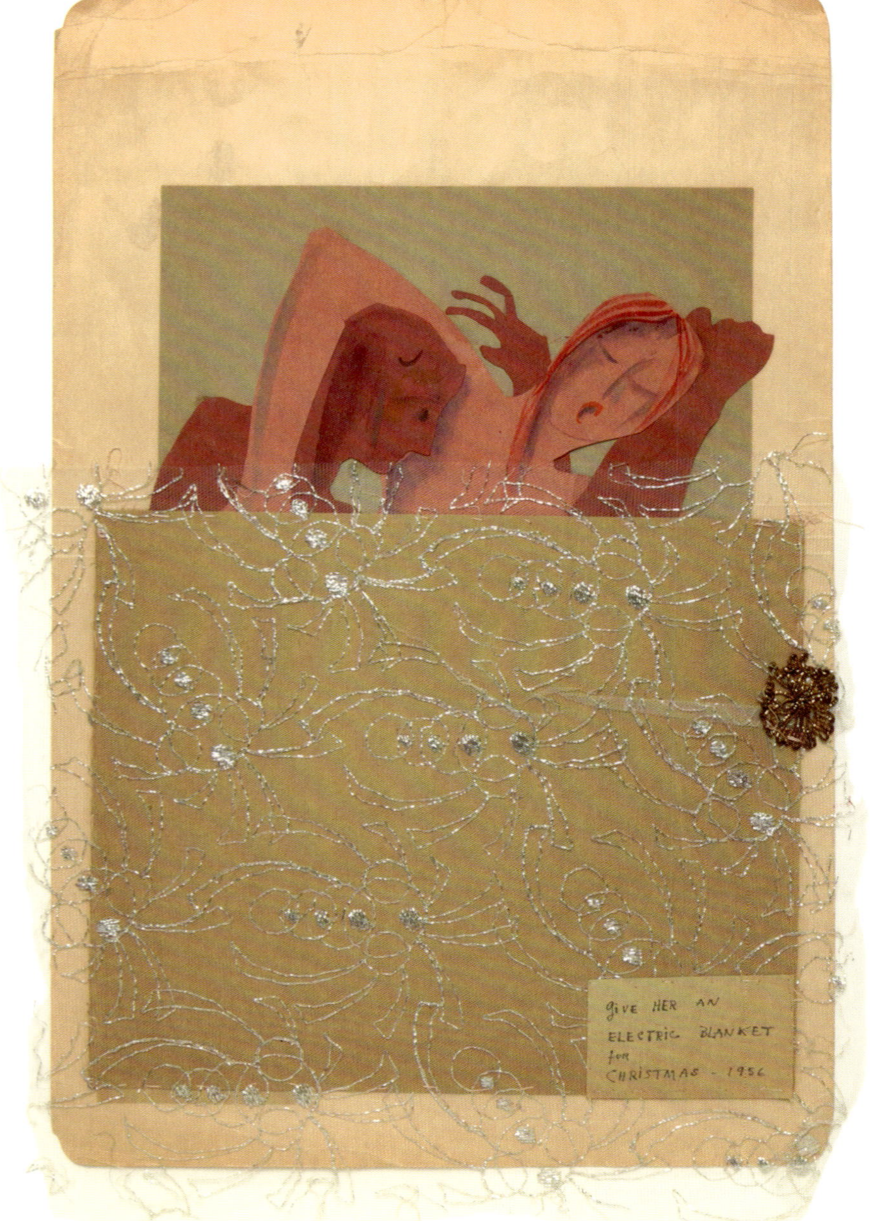

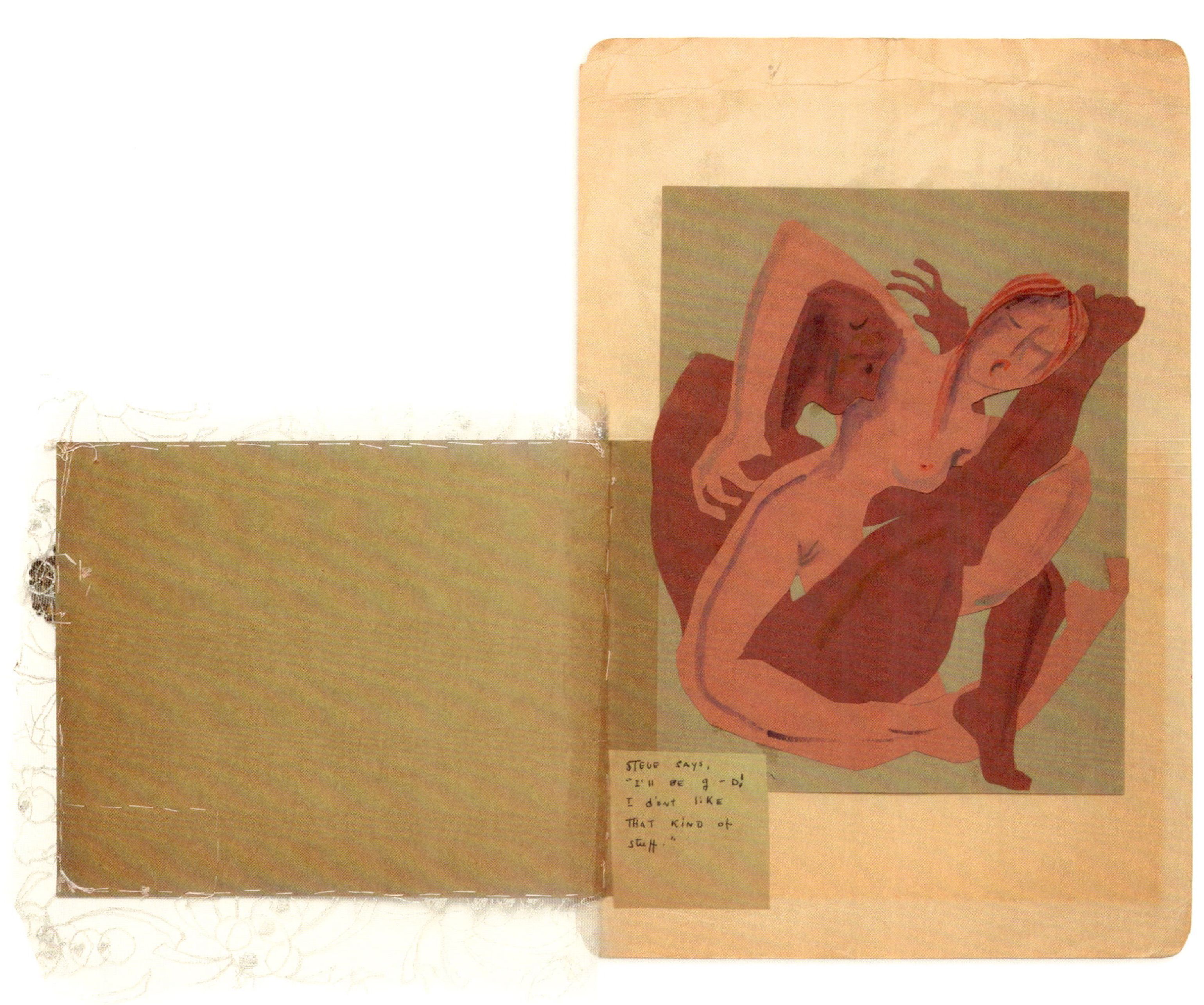

Untitled (2-page booklet), 1956, Paint, paper, and fabric collage, 18½ x 12″ (folded), 18½ x 24″ (unfolded)

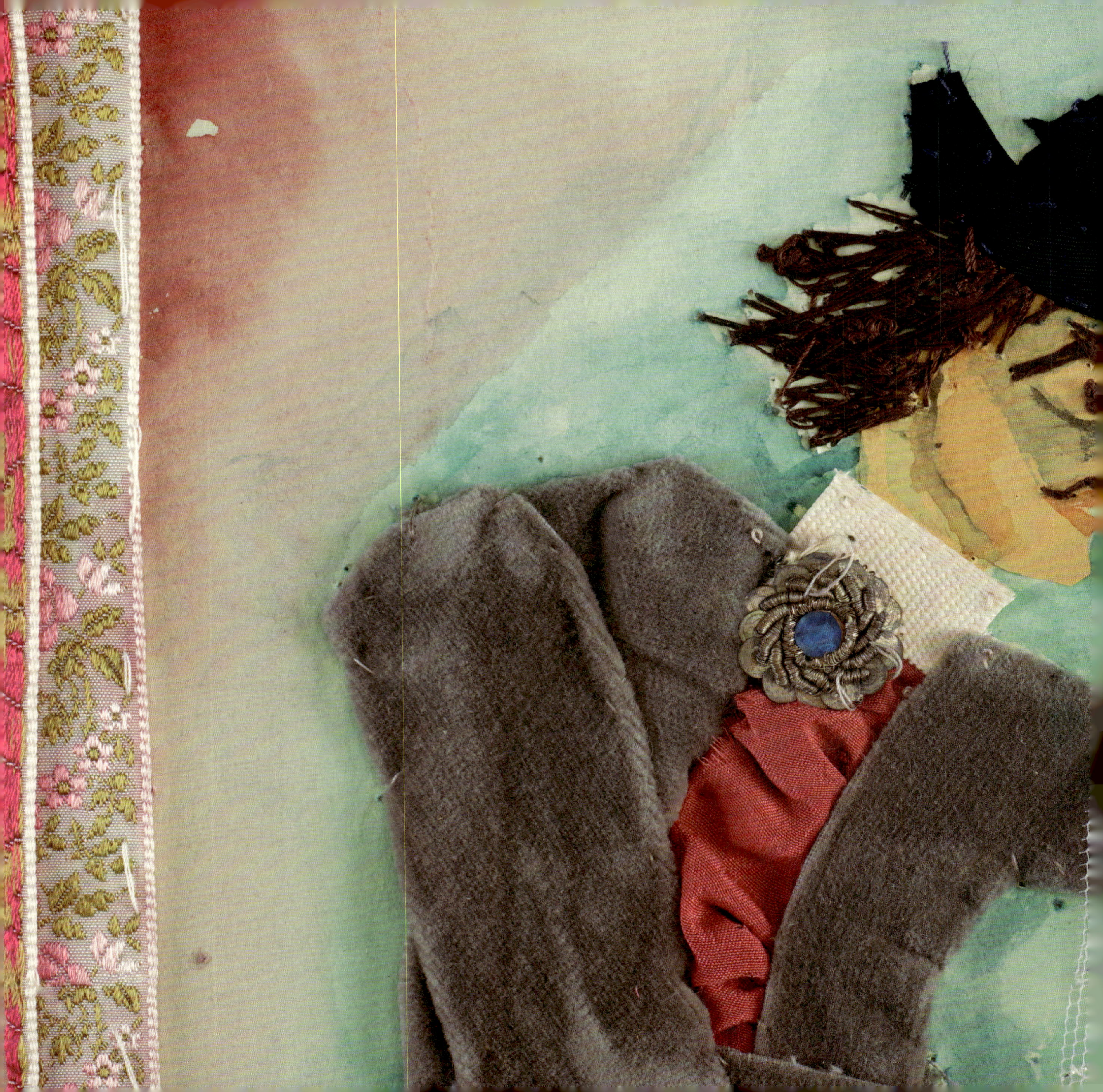

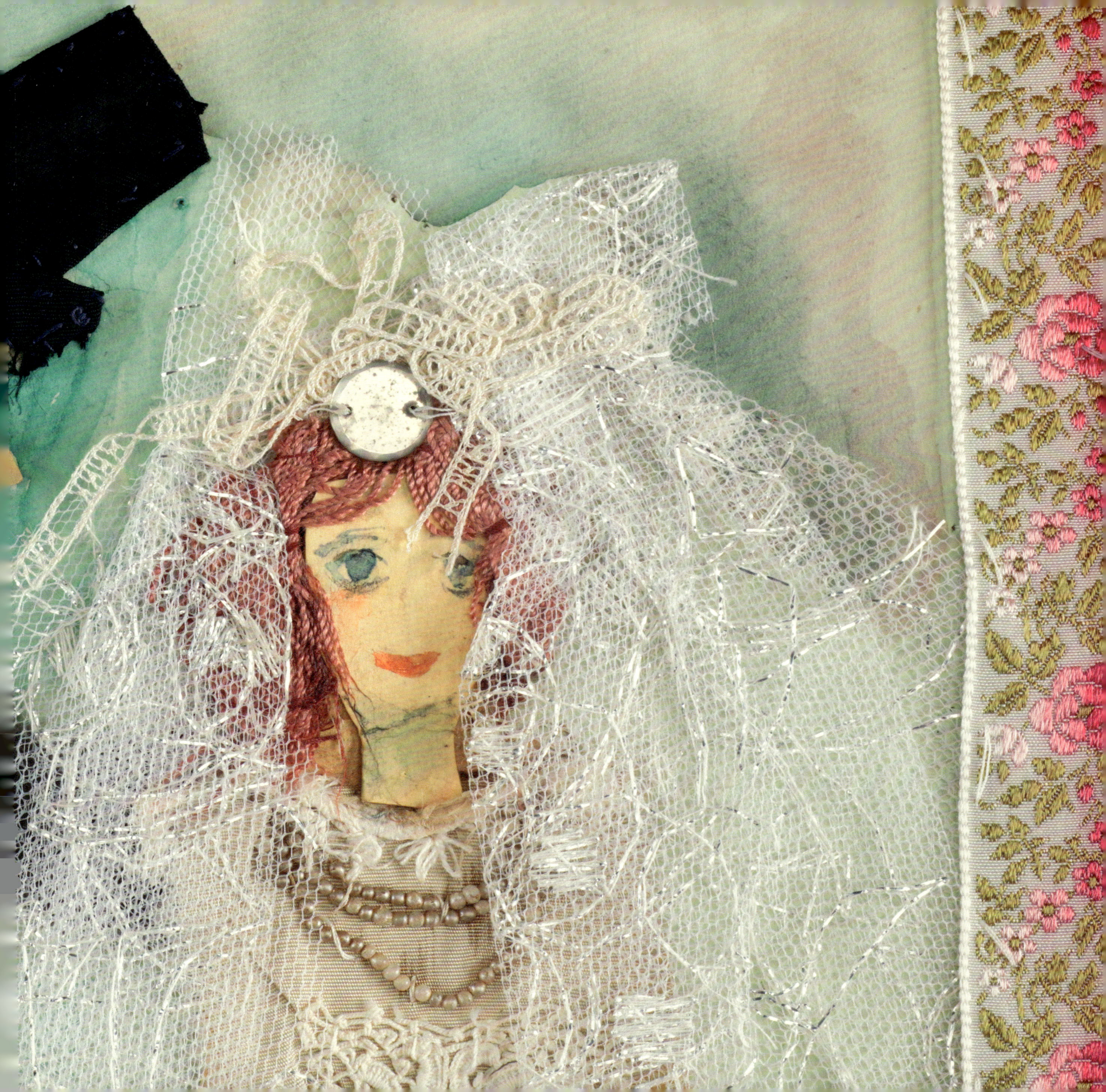

"Celebrating the marriage of Jack and Rhea Case. October 1956."

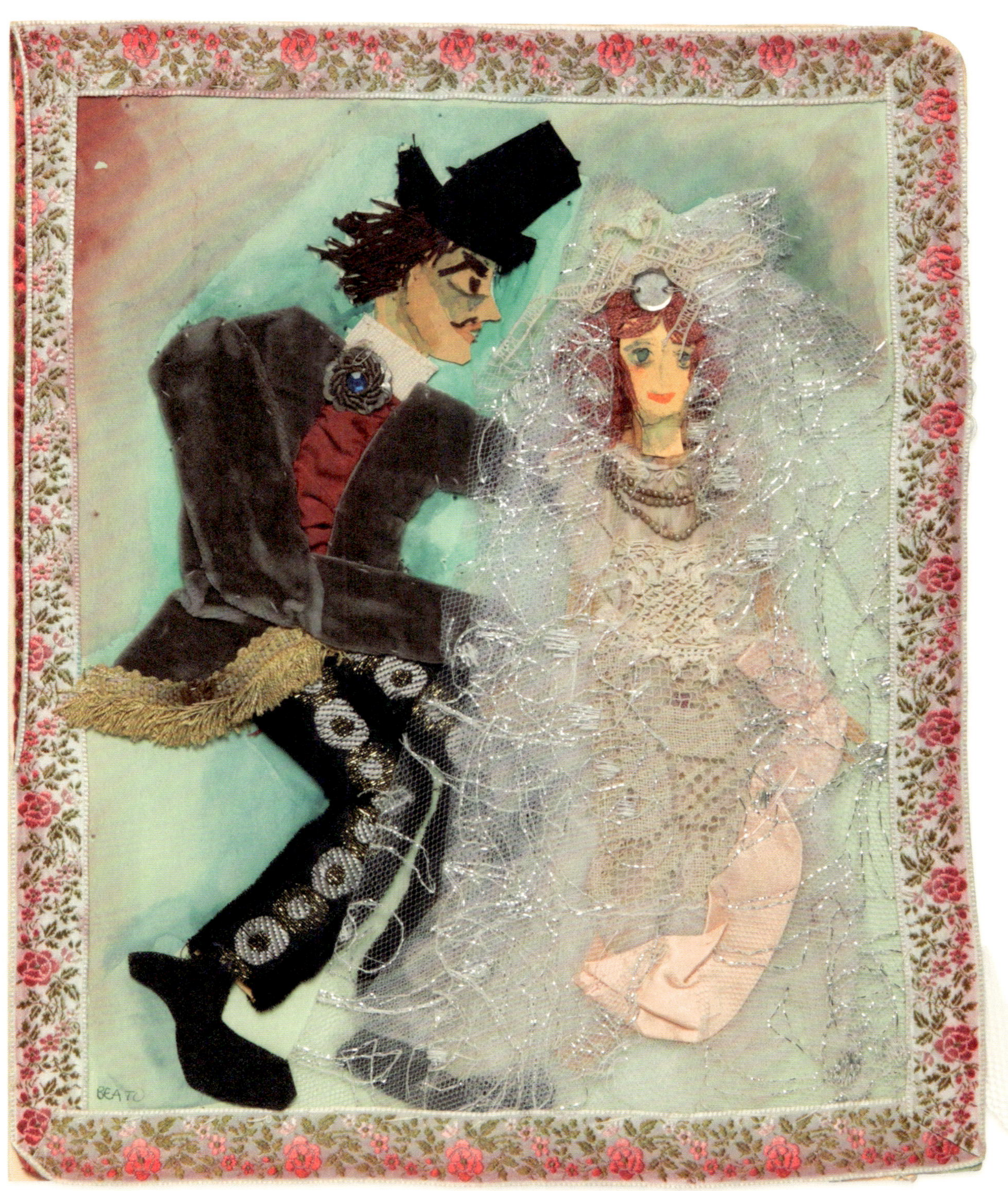

Even Kinsey Blushed, 1956, Paint, paper, and fabric collage sewn into a manila folder, 11¾ x 9¾"

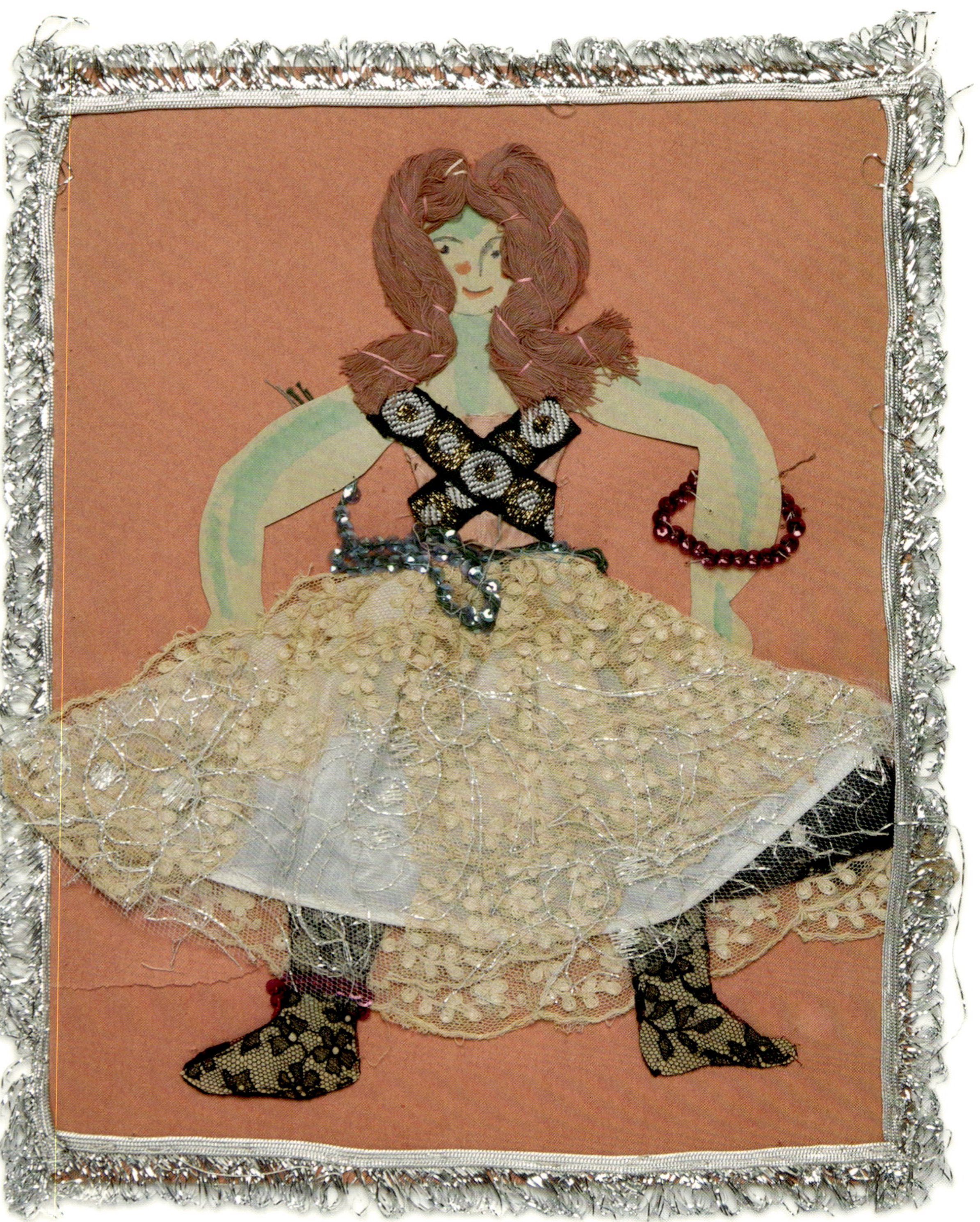

"will you be my VALENTINE?
Lift me tender,
Love me true."

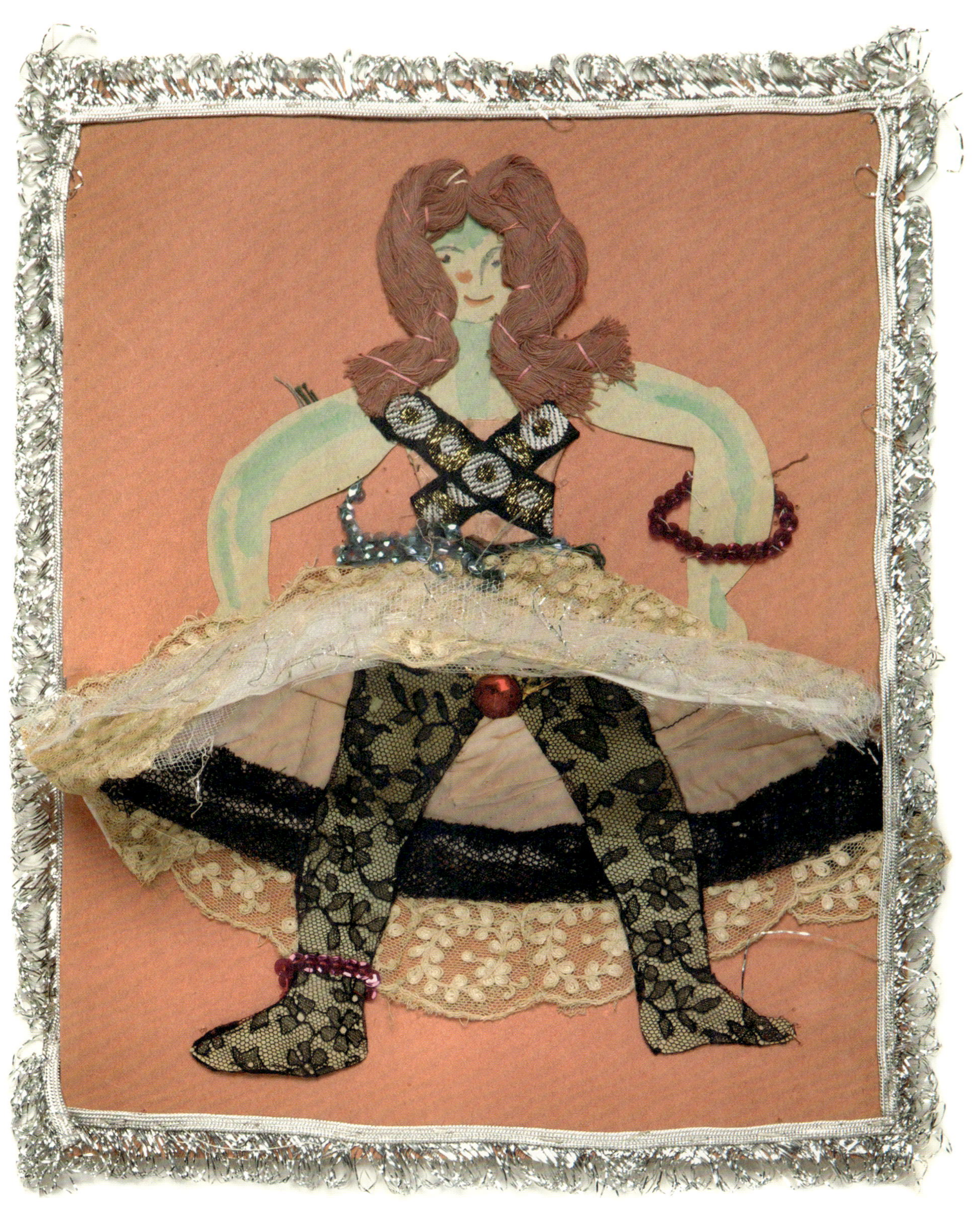

Untitled, 1957, Paper and fabric sewn into a manila folder, 12 x 10″ (folded), 12 x 20″ (unfolded)

"THE gREAT MESSAgE iNTO THE FUTURE

President Eisenhower

—THE UNRESOLVED DiPLOMATiC PROBLEM.

THE BROTHERHOOD of INTEREST

THESE KNOW WELL HOW TO TOSS A SKIRT."

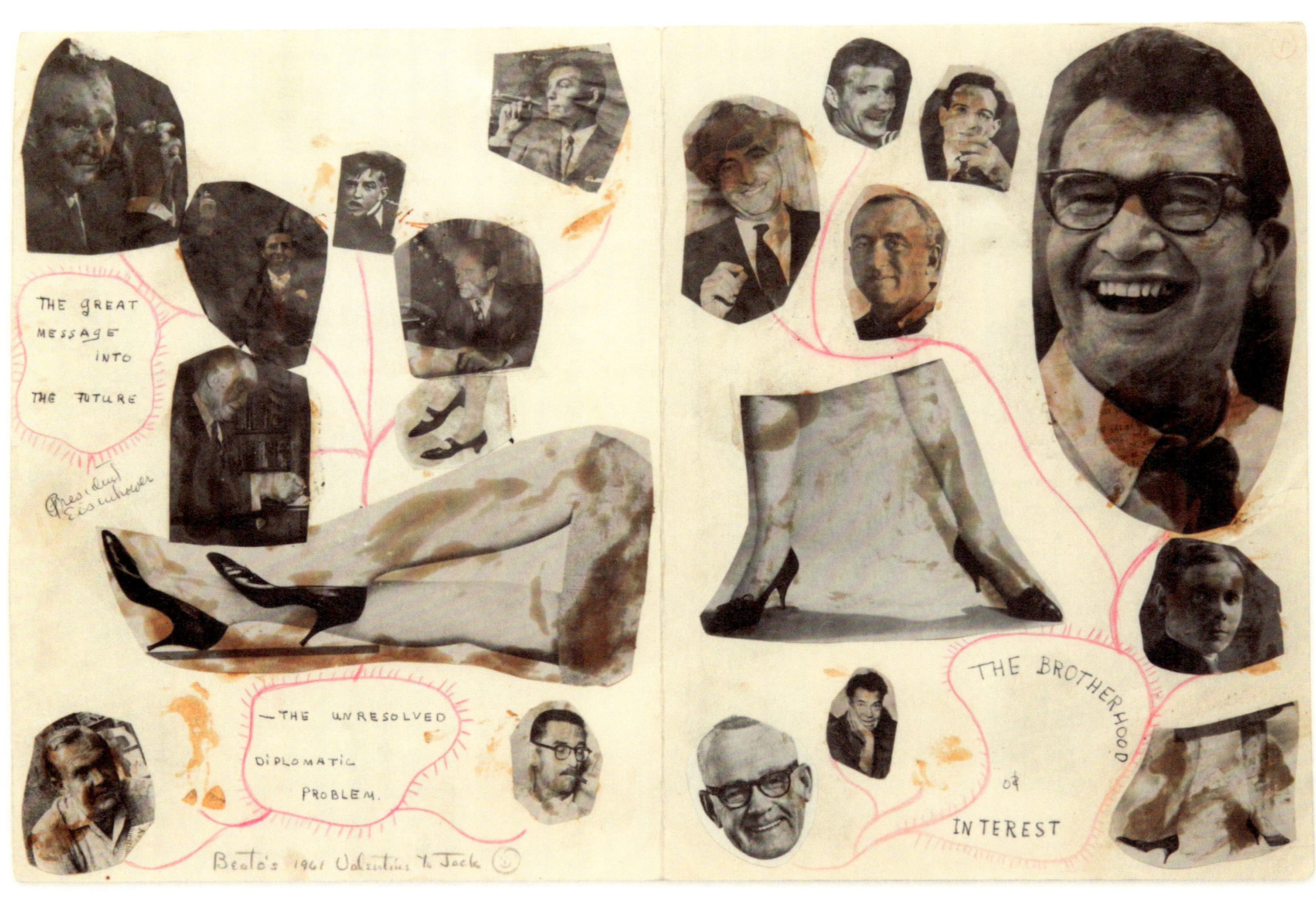

Untitled (4-page booklet), Beato's 1961 Valentine to Jack,
Undated, Paper and fabric collage, 12 x 8⁷⁄₁₀" (folded), 12 x 17" (unfolded)

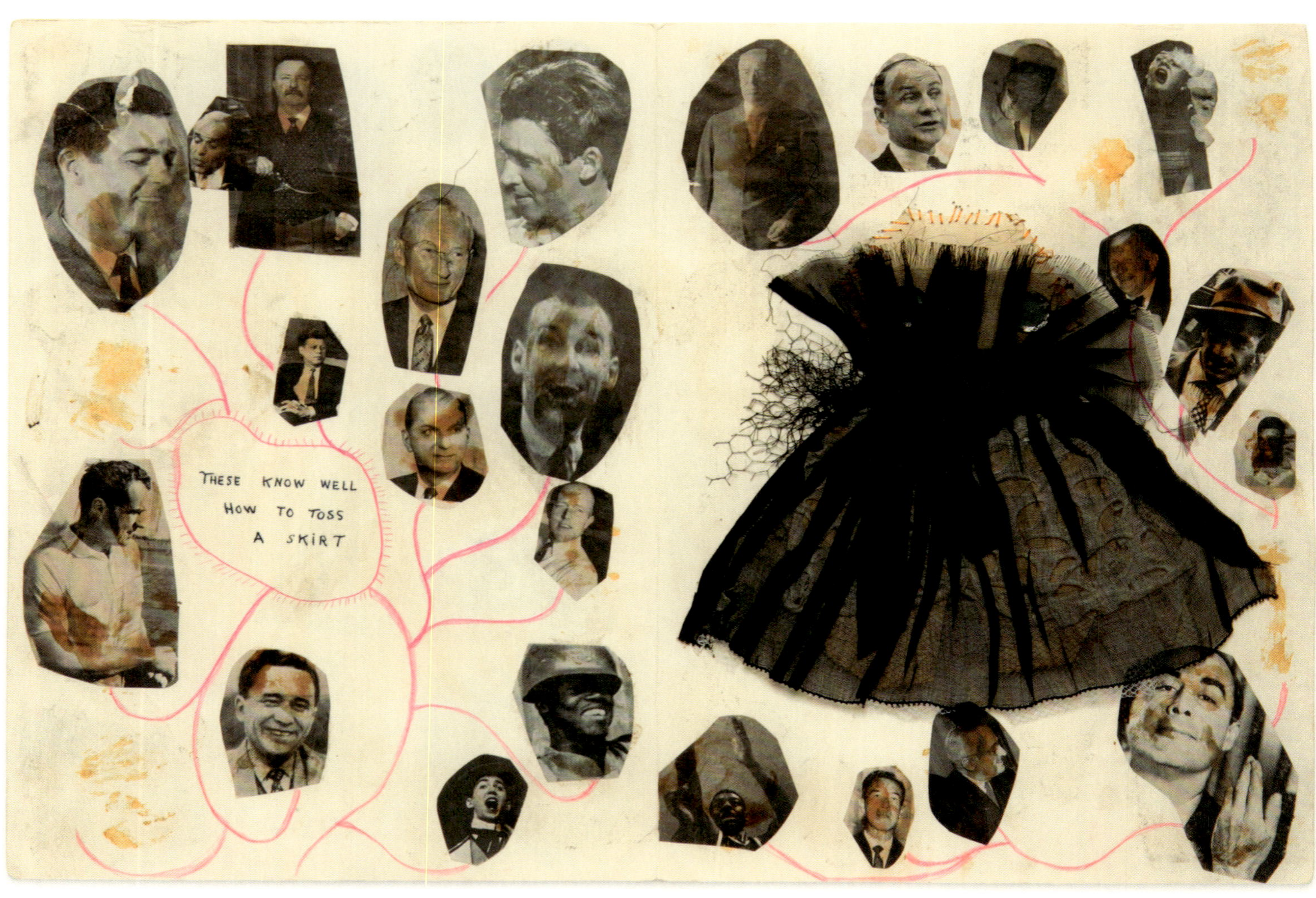
THESE KNOW WELL
HOW TO TOSS
A SKIRT

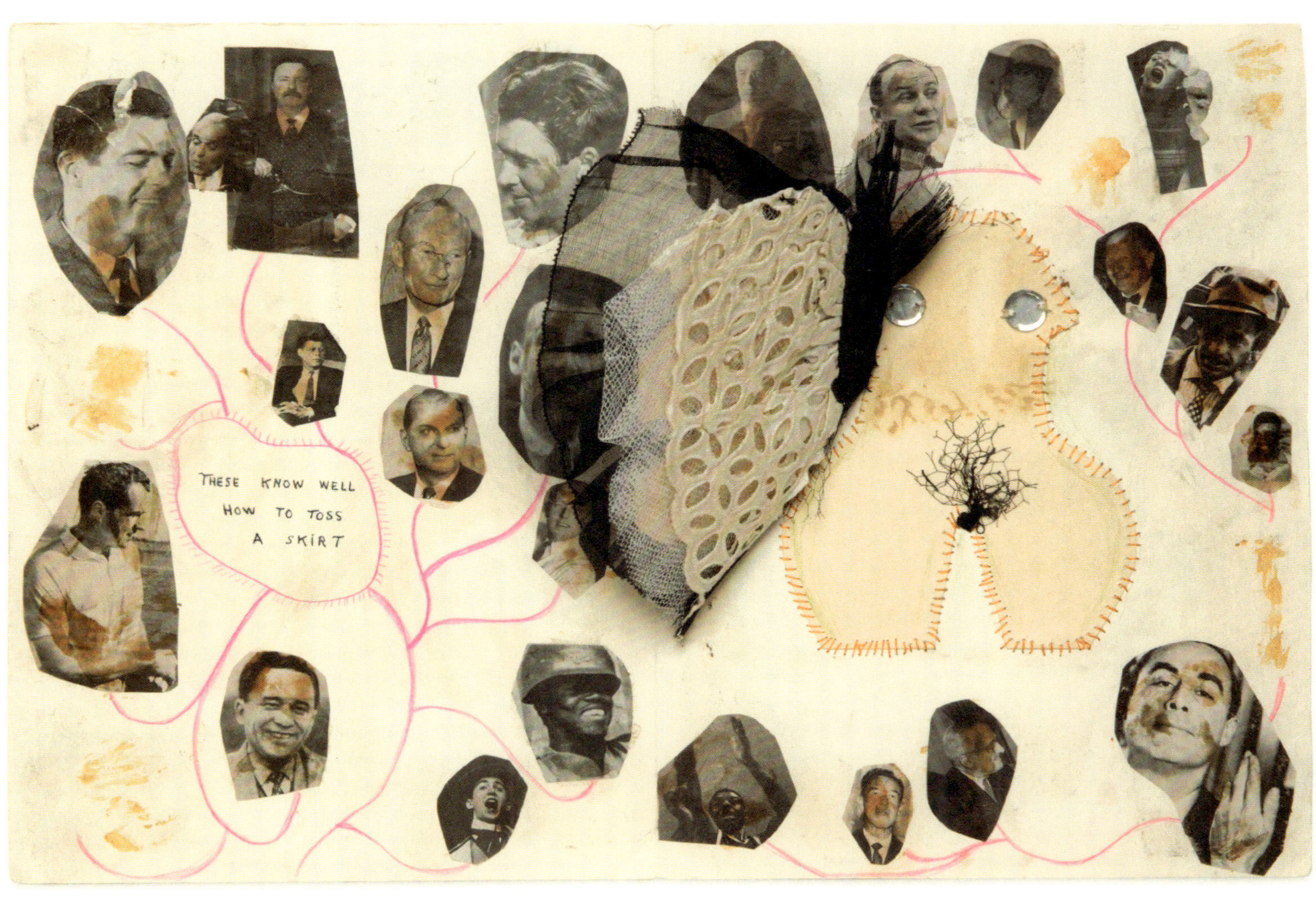

THESE KNOW WELL
HOW TO TOSS
A SKIRT

"Prelude"

"Jack wanted to know 'Prelude to what!' Poor Jack.

Happy Birthday,

Beato, 1963"

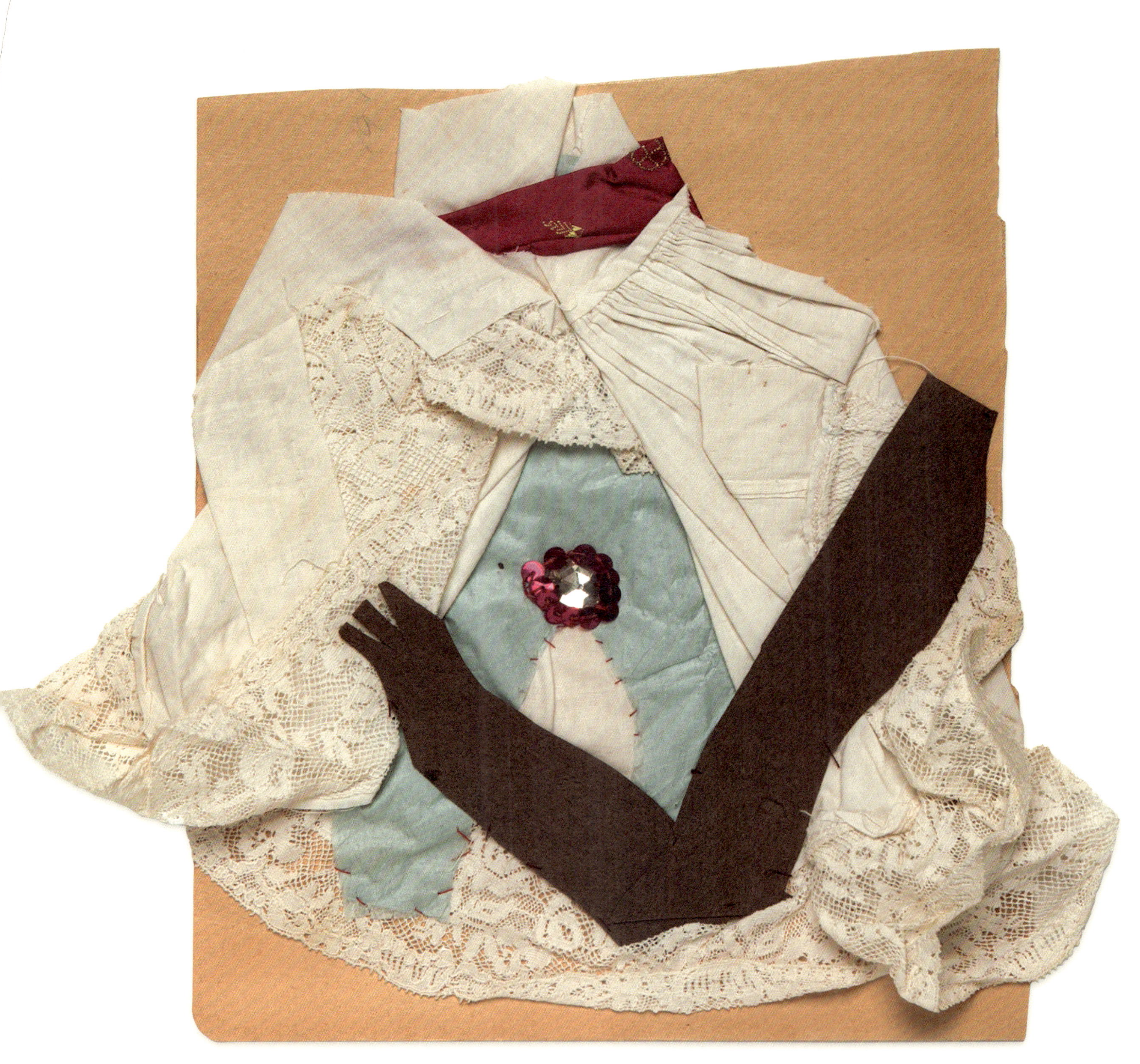

Untitled, 1963, Paper and fabric collage, 10 x 7¾"

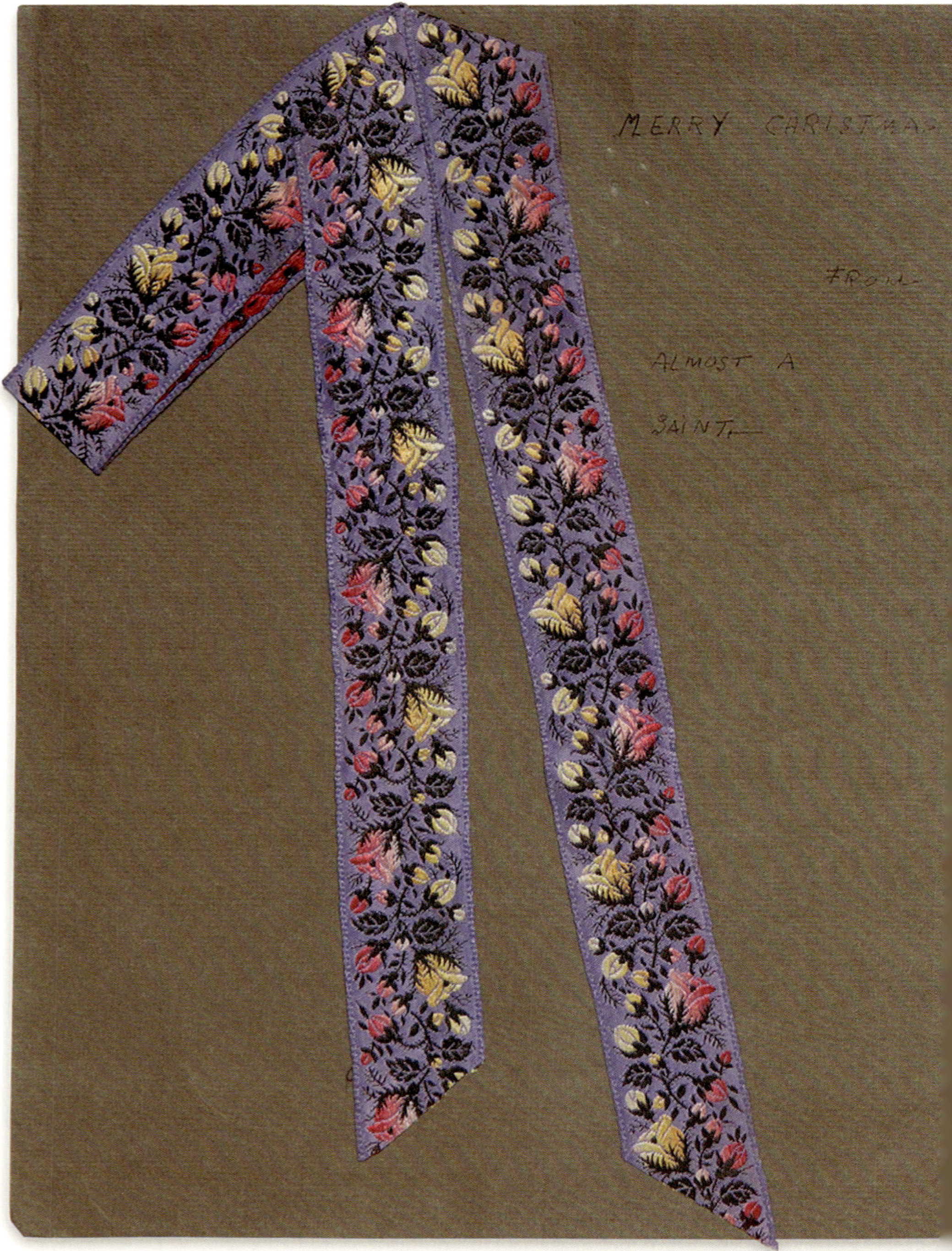

To Darling Jack and Rhea Case—Ojai—
December, 1964

"Merry Christmas from Almost a Saint—"

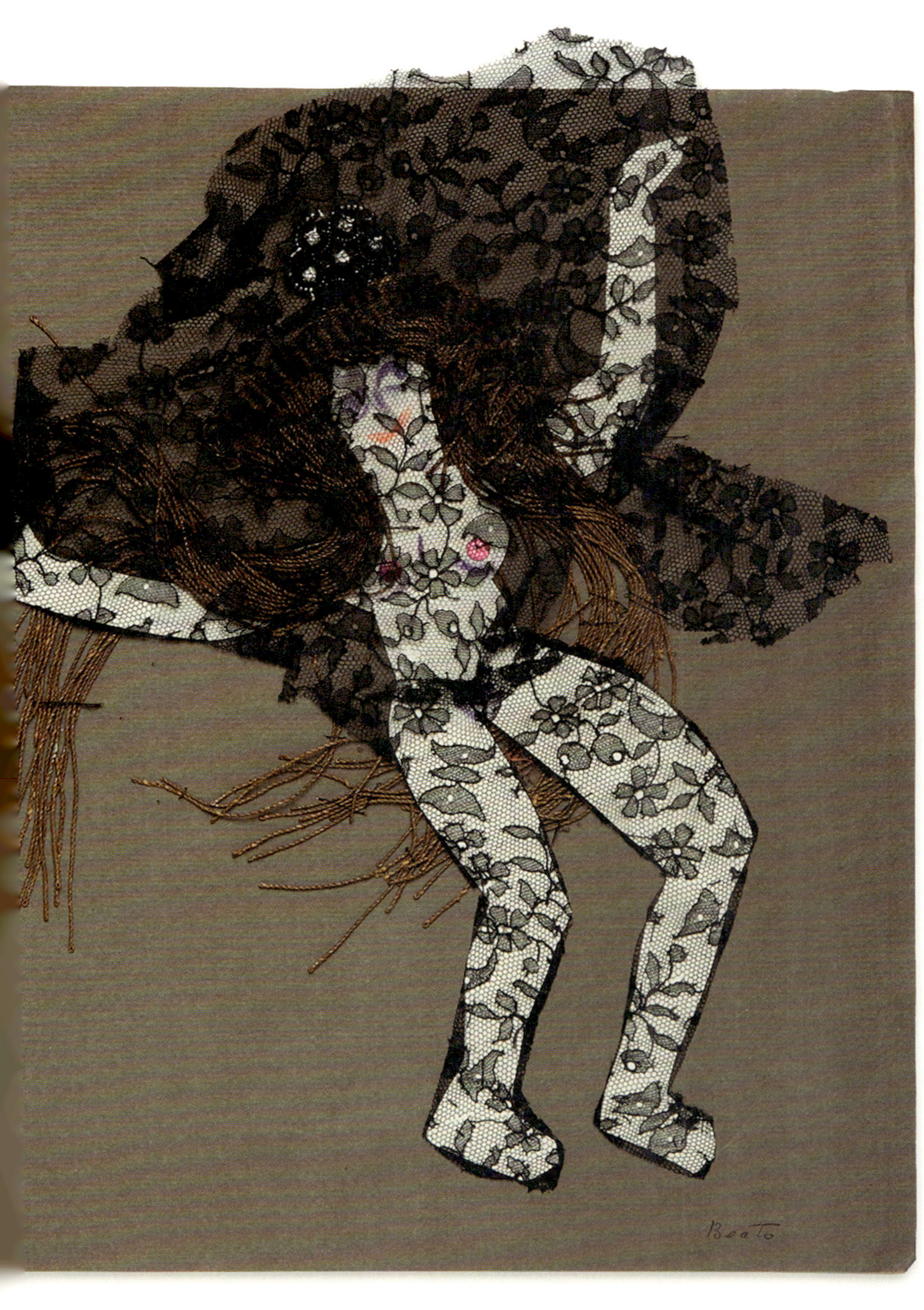

To Darling Jack and Rhea Case—Ojai—December, 1964,
Illustration, fabric, and paper collage,
12 x 9" (folded), 12 x 18" (unfolded)

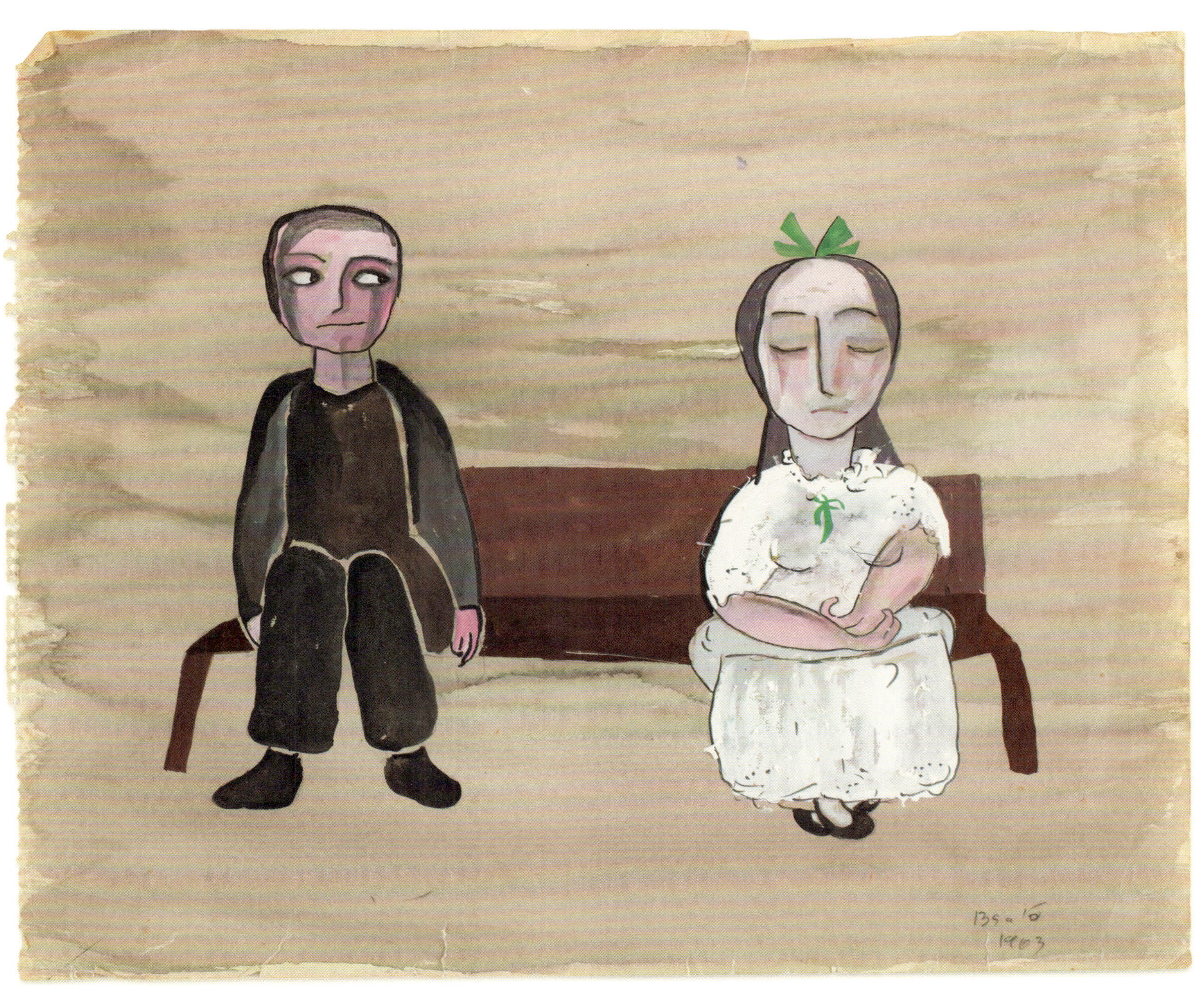

Untitled, 1963, Painting on paper, 14 x 16¾"

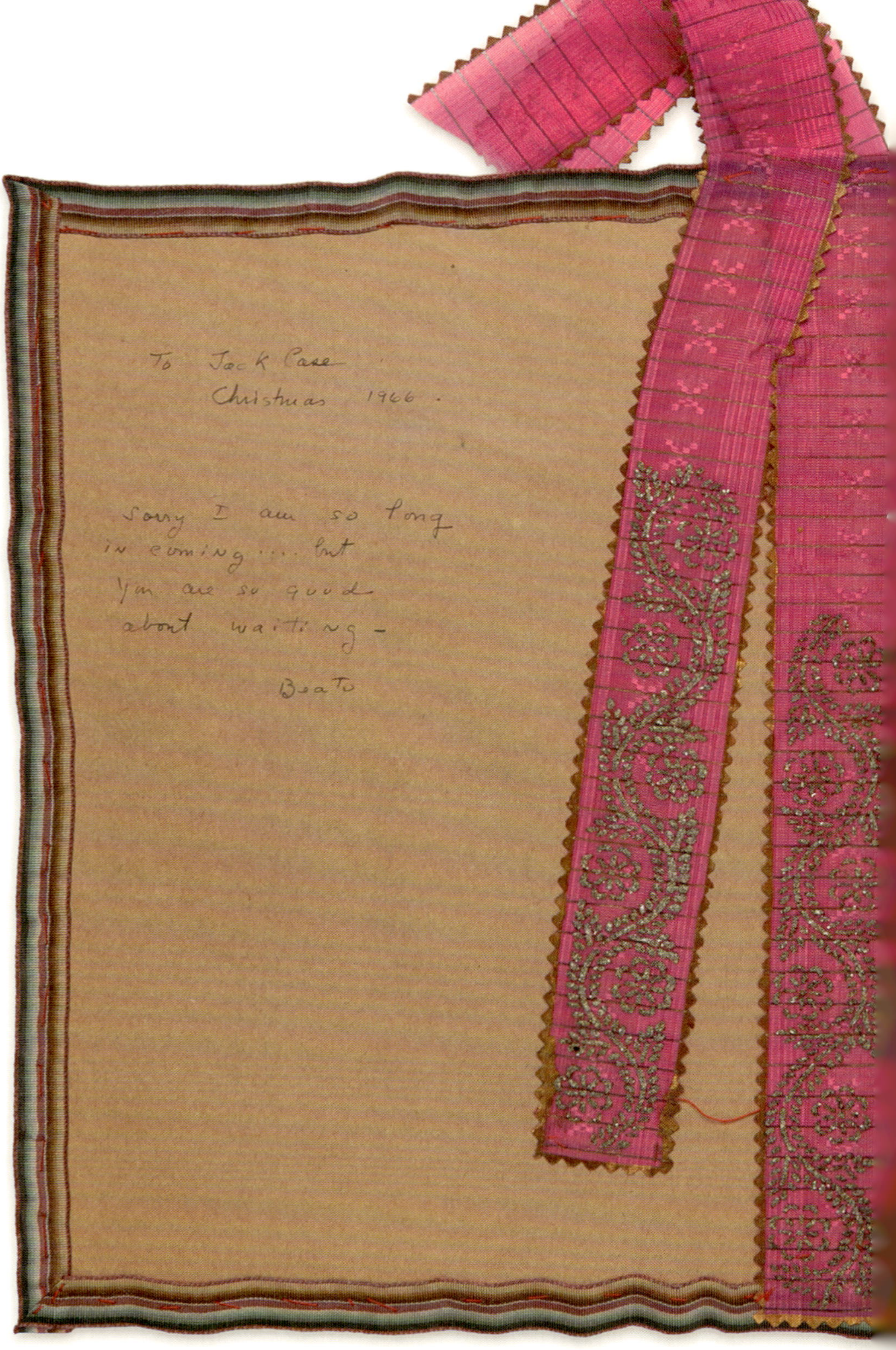

"*To Jack Case, Christmas 1966*

Sorry I am so long in coming…
but you are so good about waiting—

Beato

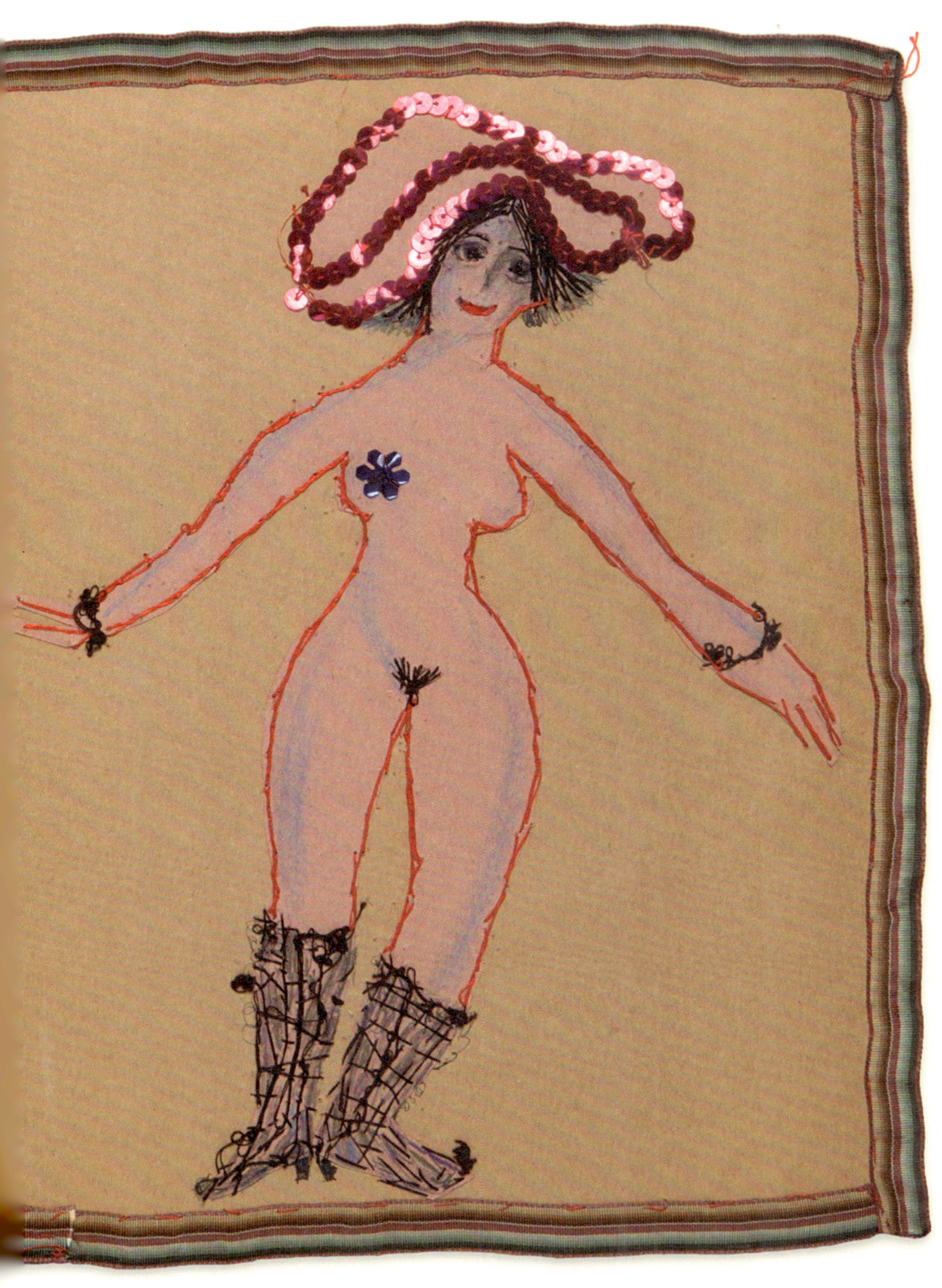

Untitled, 1966, Paper and fabric collage, 12 x 18½"

"Season's Greetings from the Left Bubby—1973"

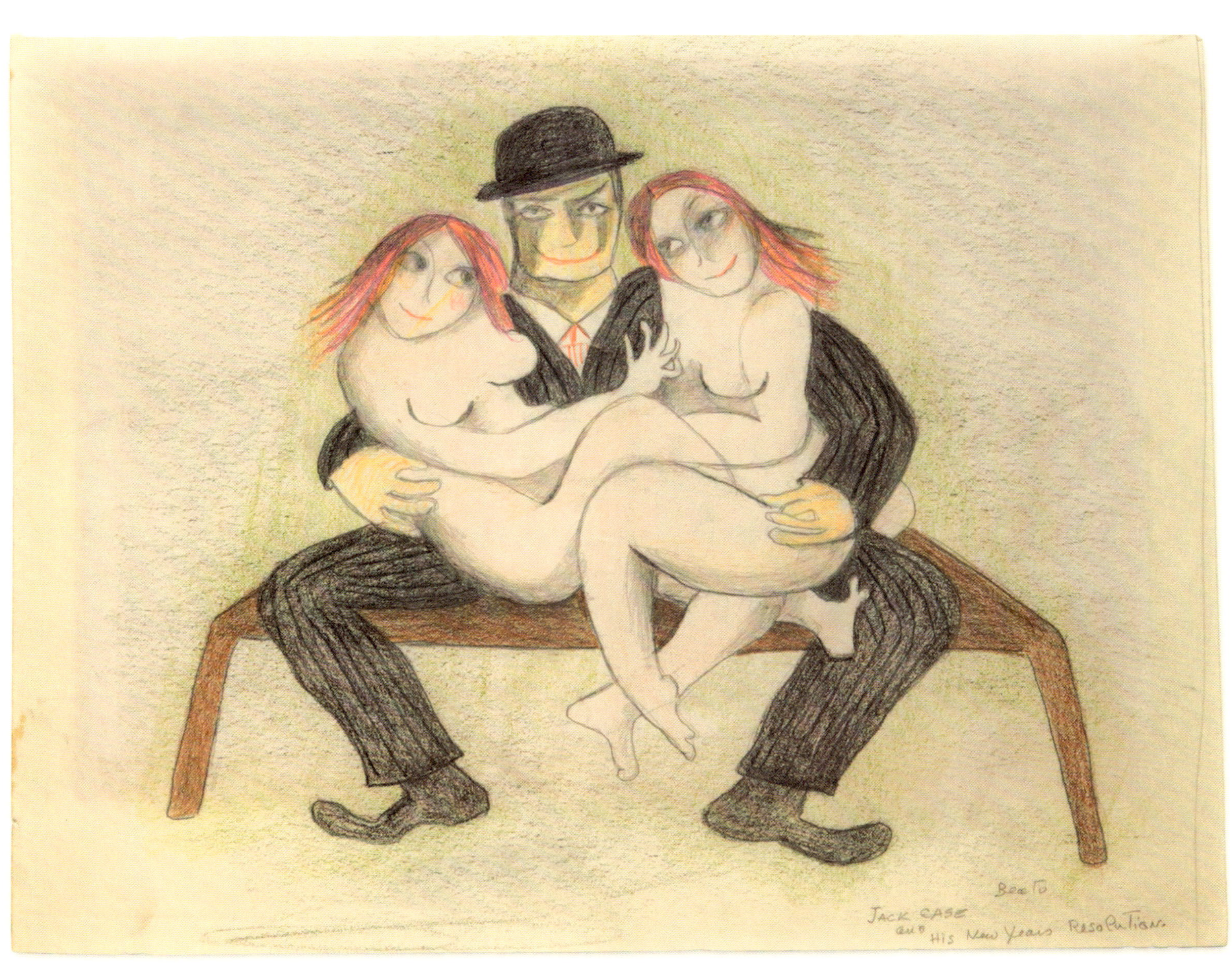

JACK CASE and His New Years Resolution, Undated, Illustration on paper, 9½ x 12½"

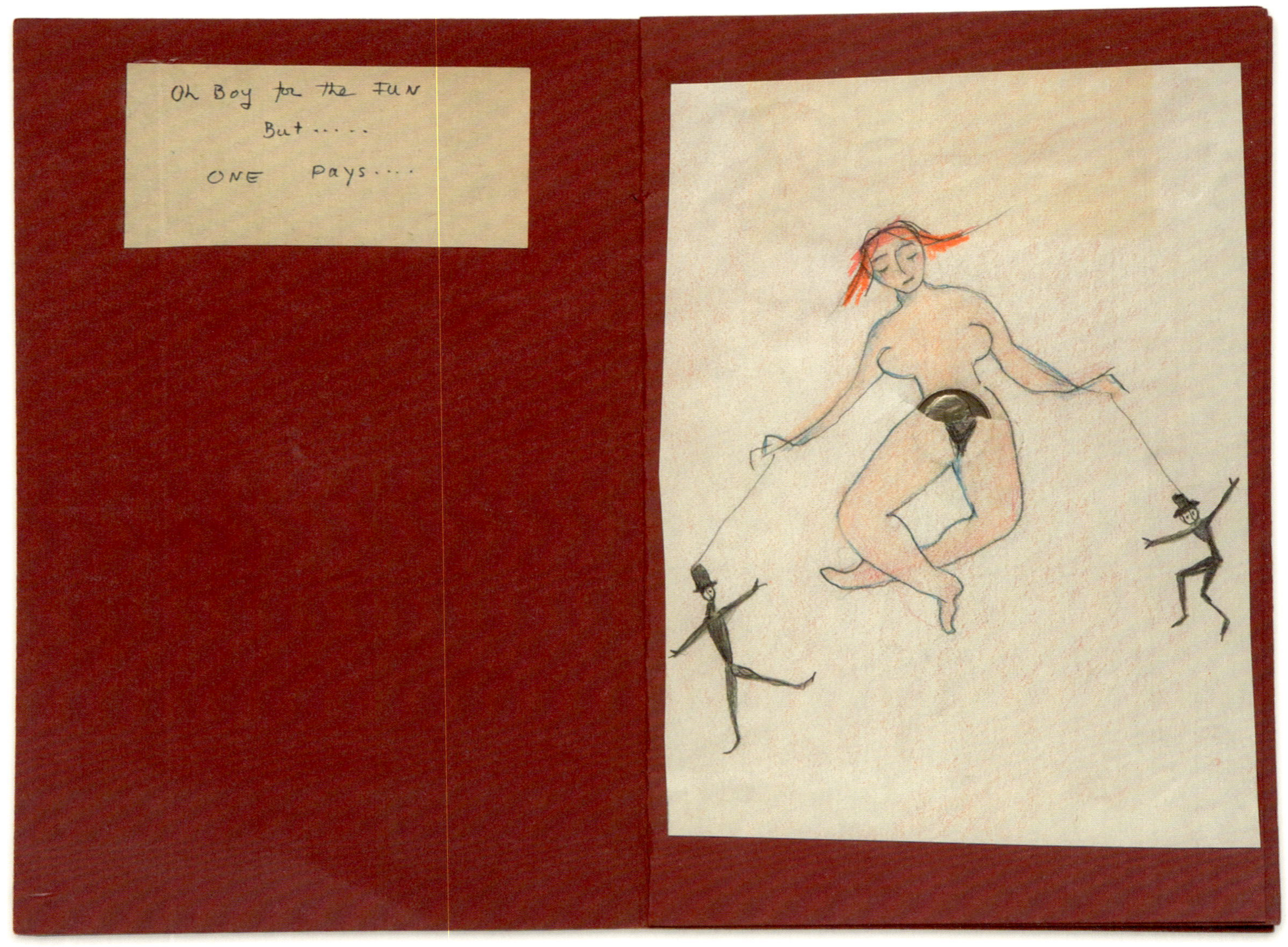

"Oh Boy for the FUN

But.....

ONE Pays....,

Except Jack for whom it is always FREE....."

 "MERRY CHRISTMAS... 1974 To the IRRISTABLE JACK CASE From Loving BEATO."

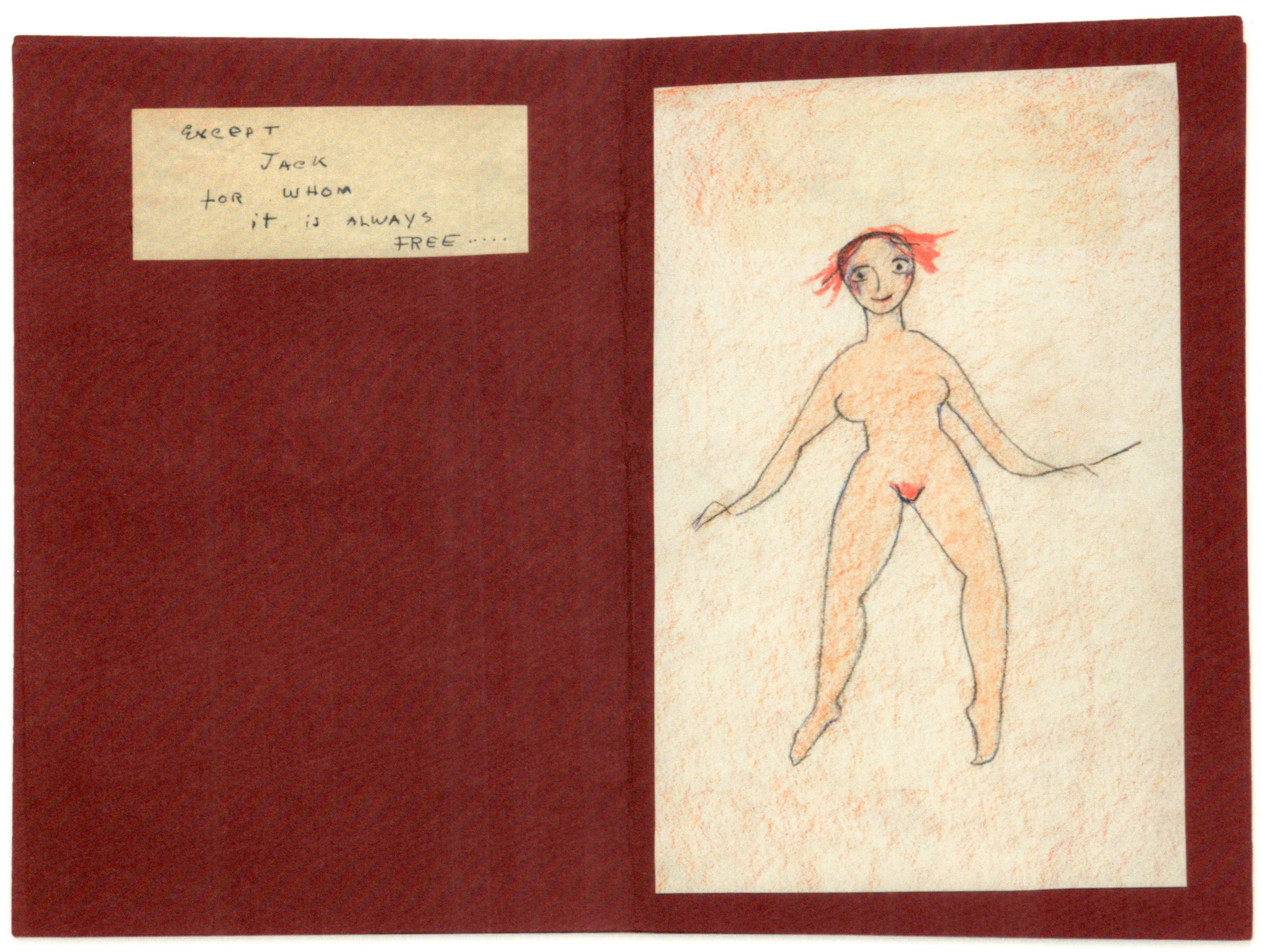

Untitled (8-page booklet), Undated, Illustration on paper, 8 ⅕ x 5½" (folded), 8 ⅕ x 11" (unfolded)

"god-dAM BEDPAN,

god-dAM HOSPiTAL,

god-dAM soN ata BiTCH HERNia.

.... Oh, hello EVERYBODY! / MERRY CHRISTMAS."

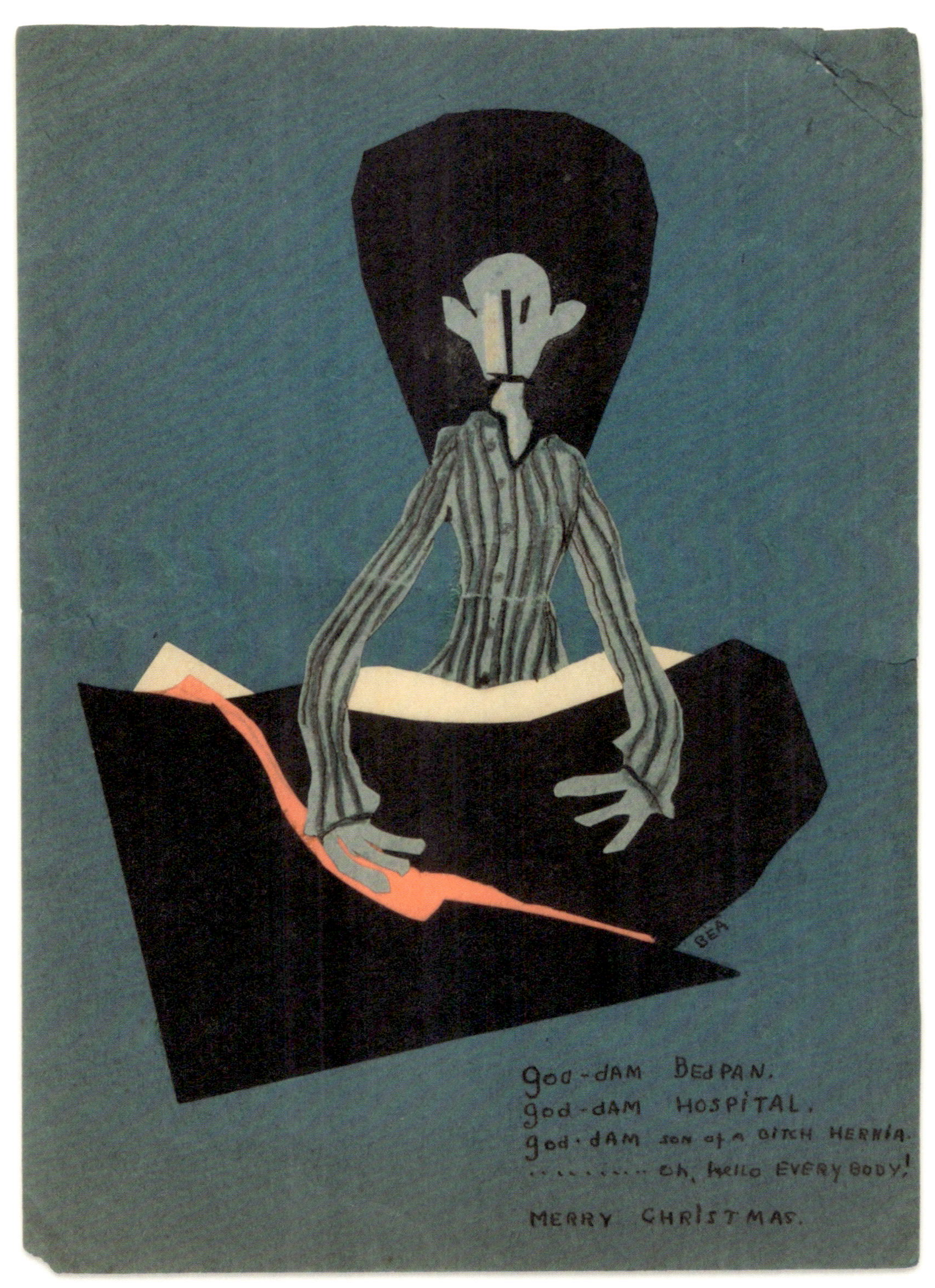

Untitled, Undated, Paper collage, 10¼ x 7¼"

*"Some Rike Ride on horseback
Some Rike Ride on burro
I Rike Ride on brussing bride
Arse prop up on piro"*

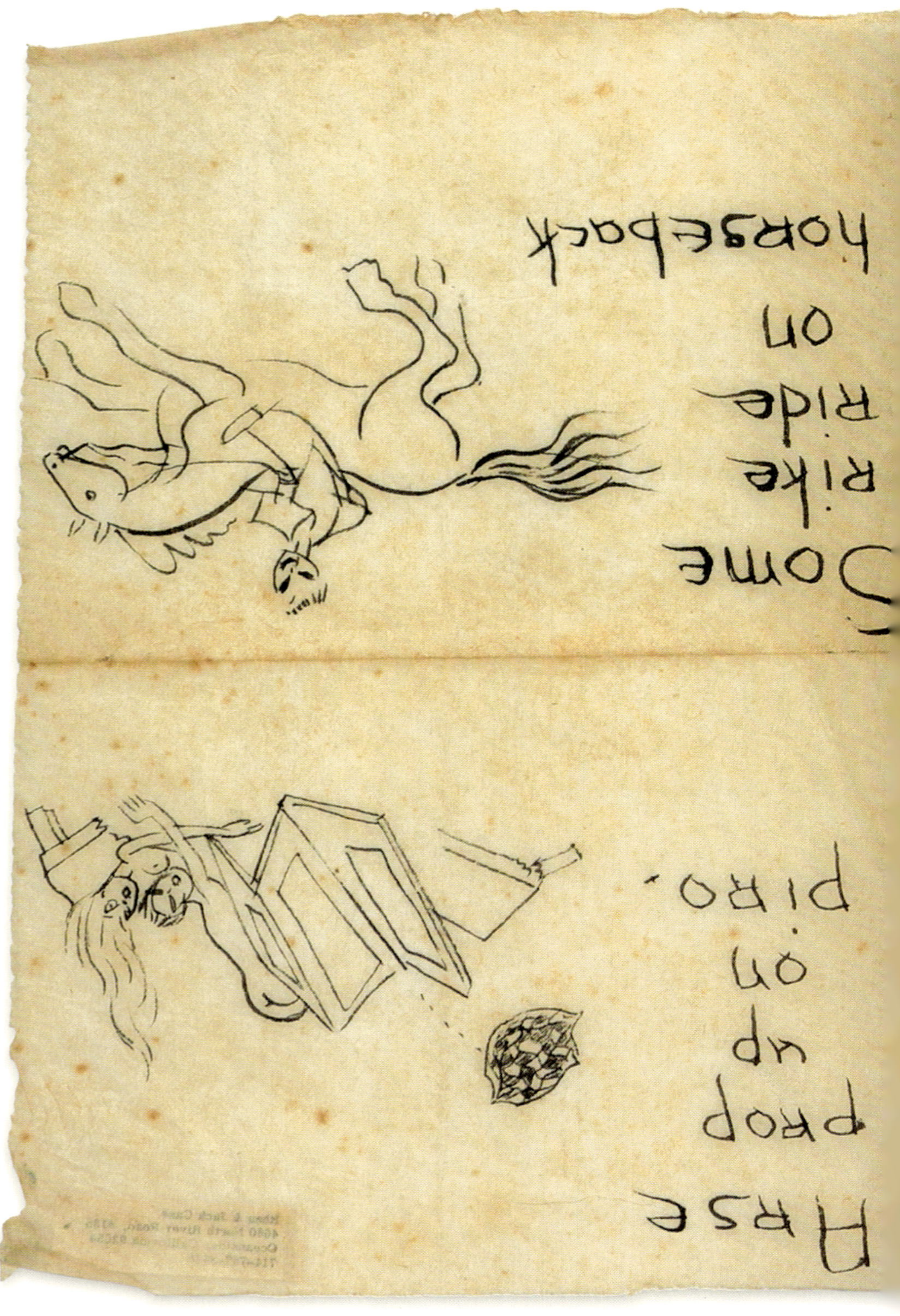

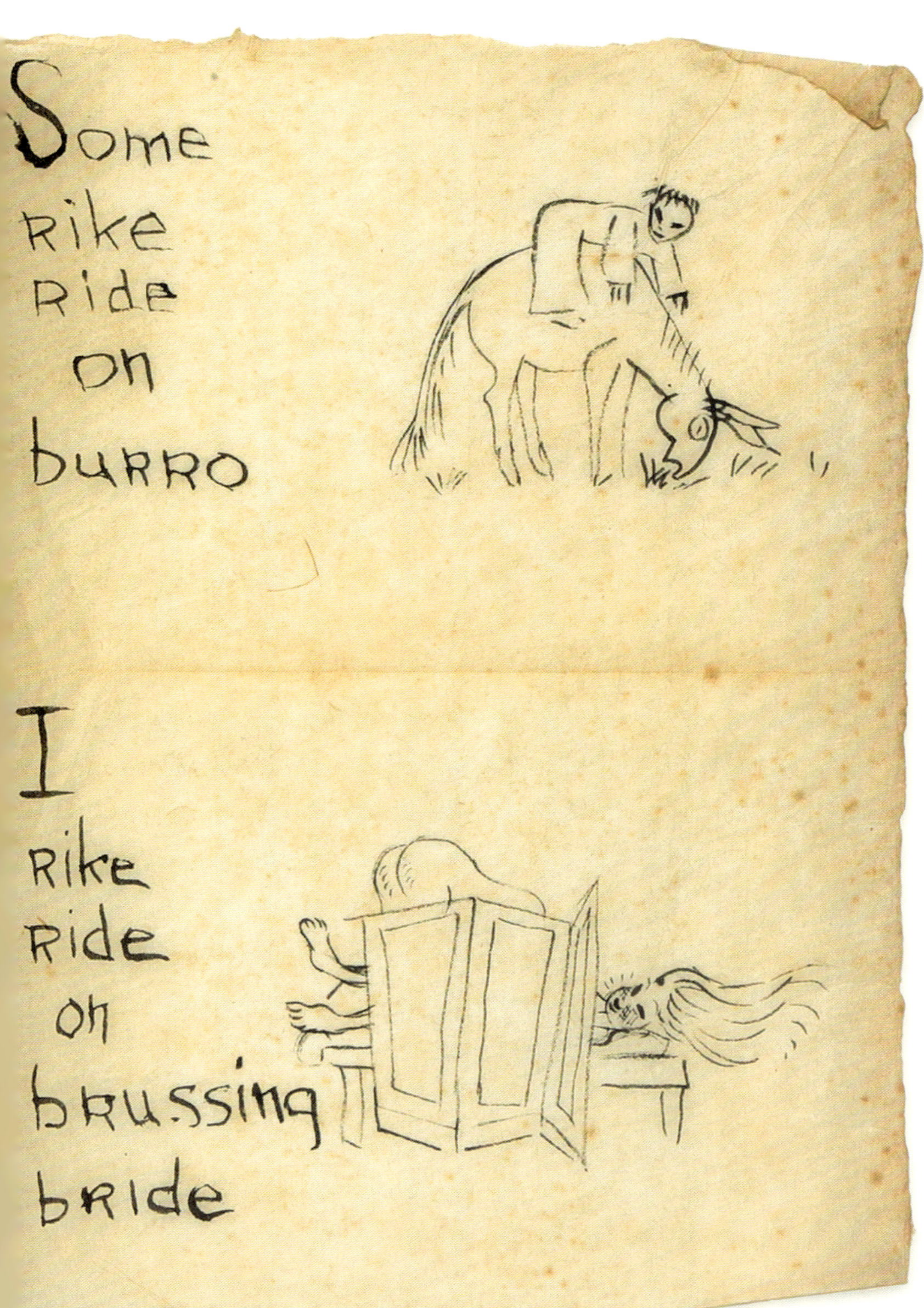

Untitled, Undated, Illustration on 4-fold paper, 4½ x 6¼″ (folded), 9 x 12½″ (unfolded)

Thank you for teaching me Japanese

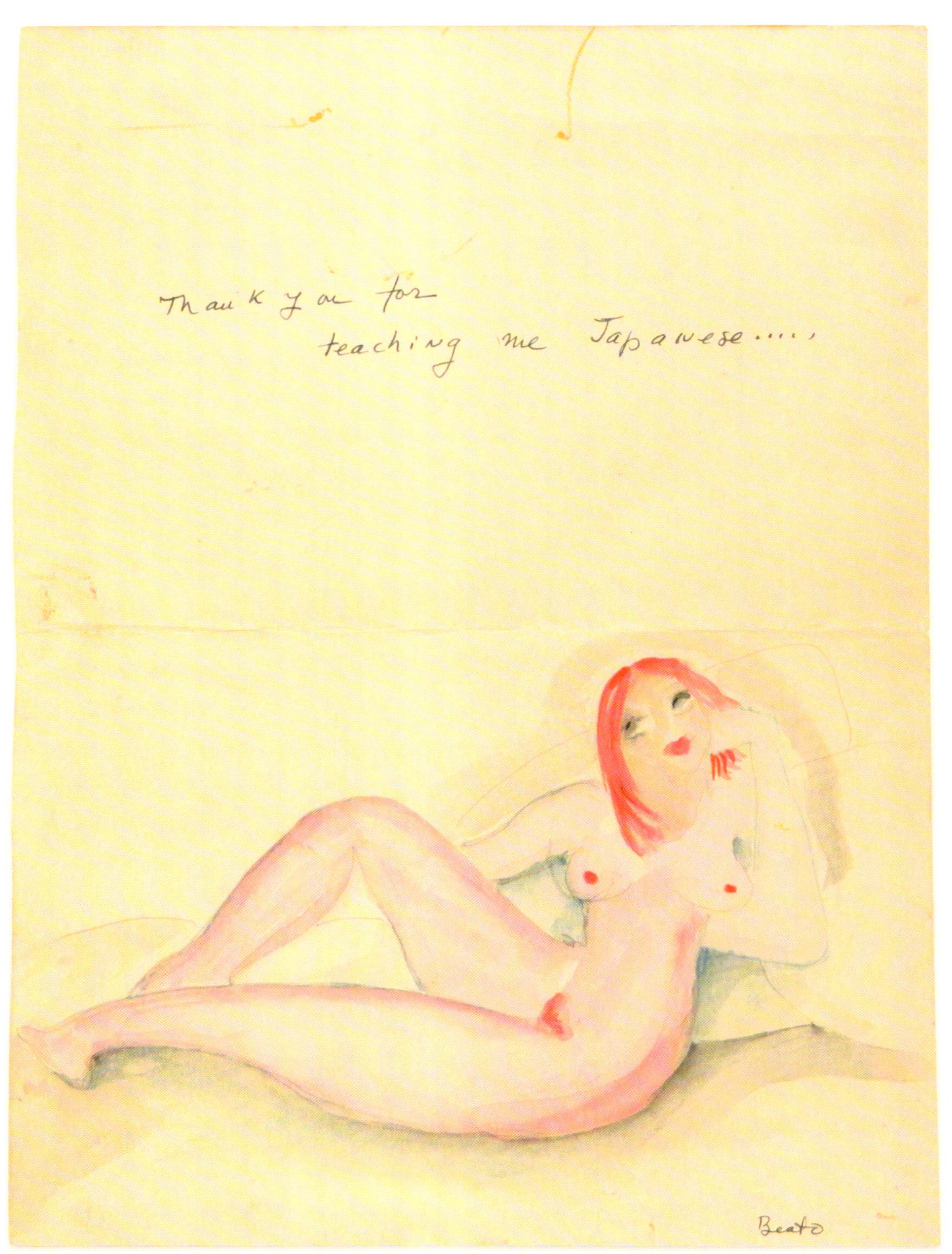

Thank you for teaching me Japanese, Undated, Illustration on paper, 12 x 8¾"

Oh, No, No. No!

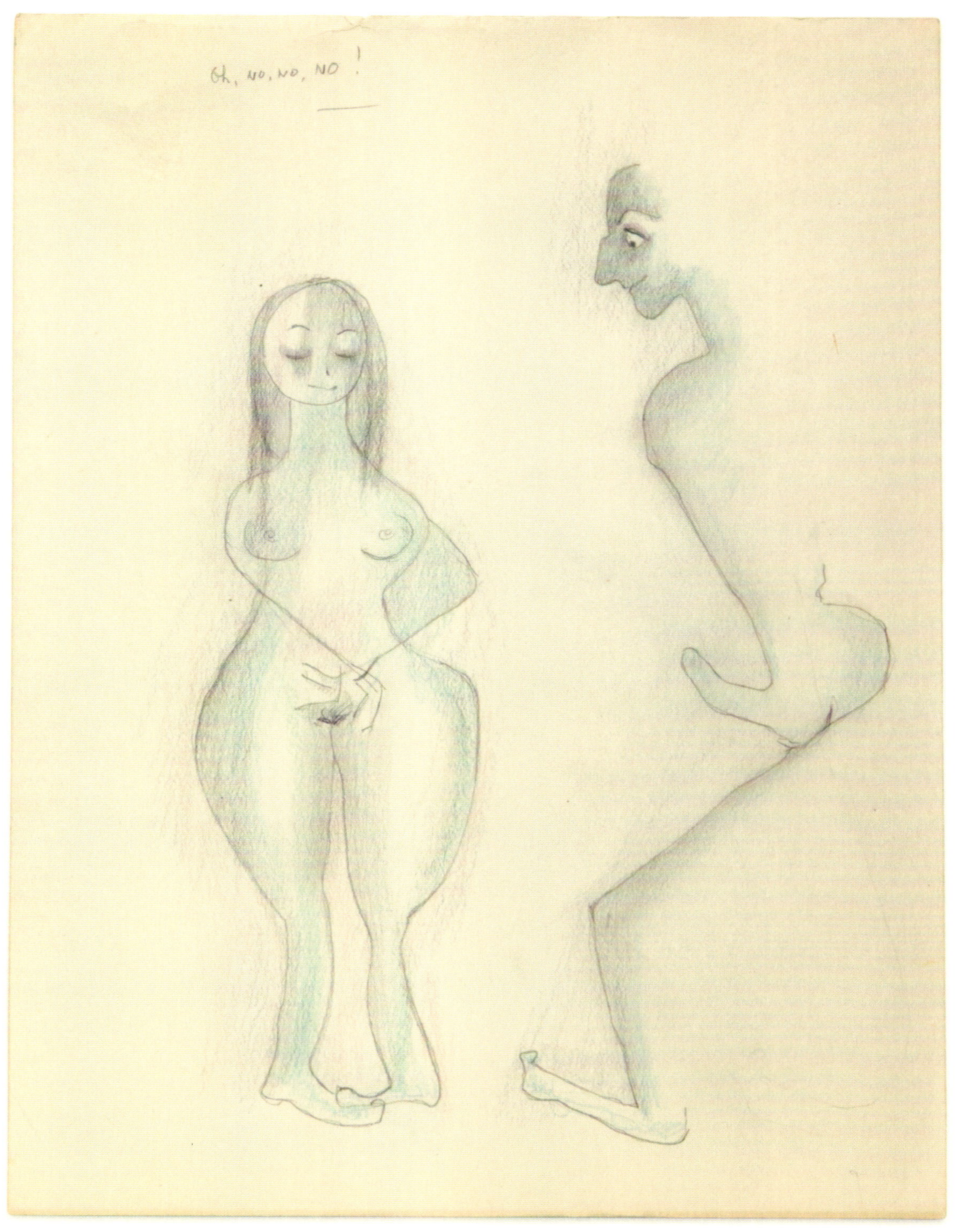

Oh, No, No. No!, Undated, Illustration on paper, 12 x 9″

Oh, YES, YES, YES!

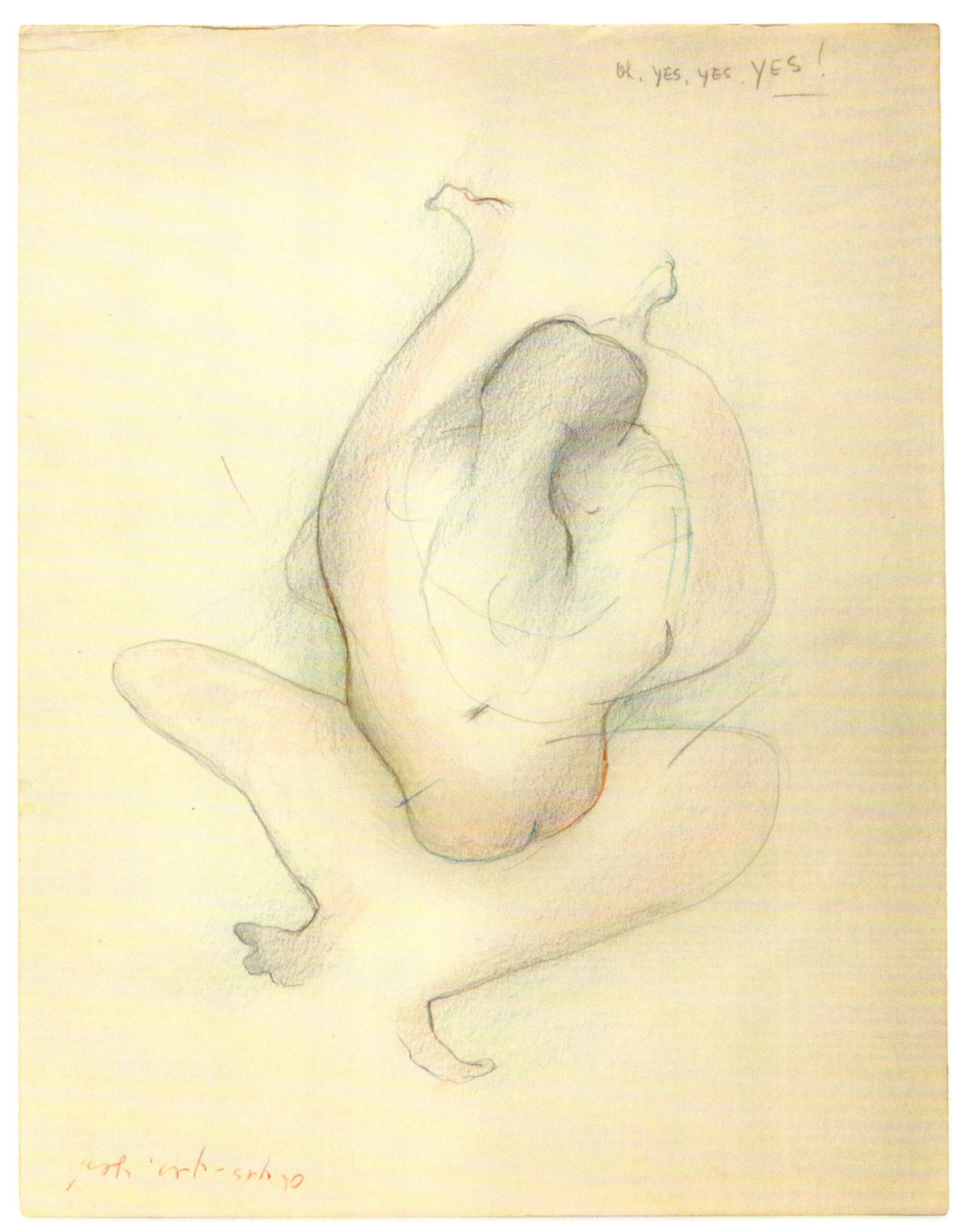

Oh, YES, YES, YES!, Undated, Illustration on paper, 12 x 9″

WE ARE SO GLAD IT is ONLY YOUR TOE THAT iS BROKEN

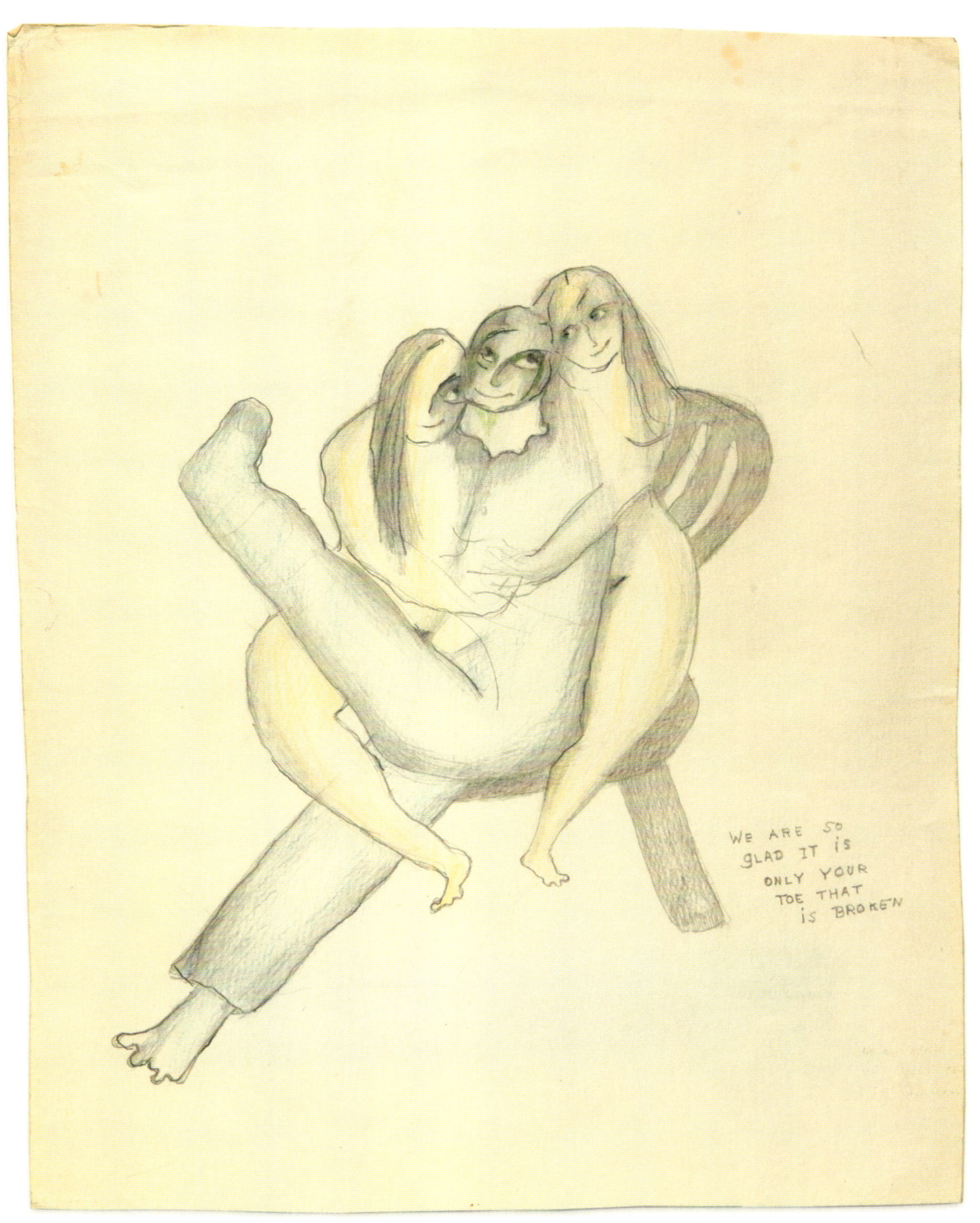

WE ARE SO GLAD IT is ONLY YOUR TOE THAT iS BROKEN, Undated, Illustration on paper, 16¼ x 12¹⁄₁₀"

"Will You Be My Valentine?"

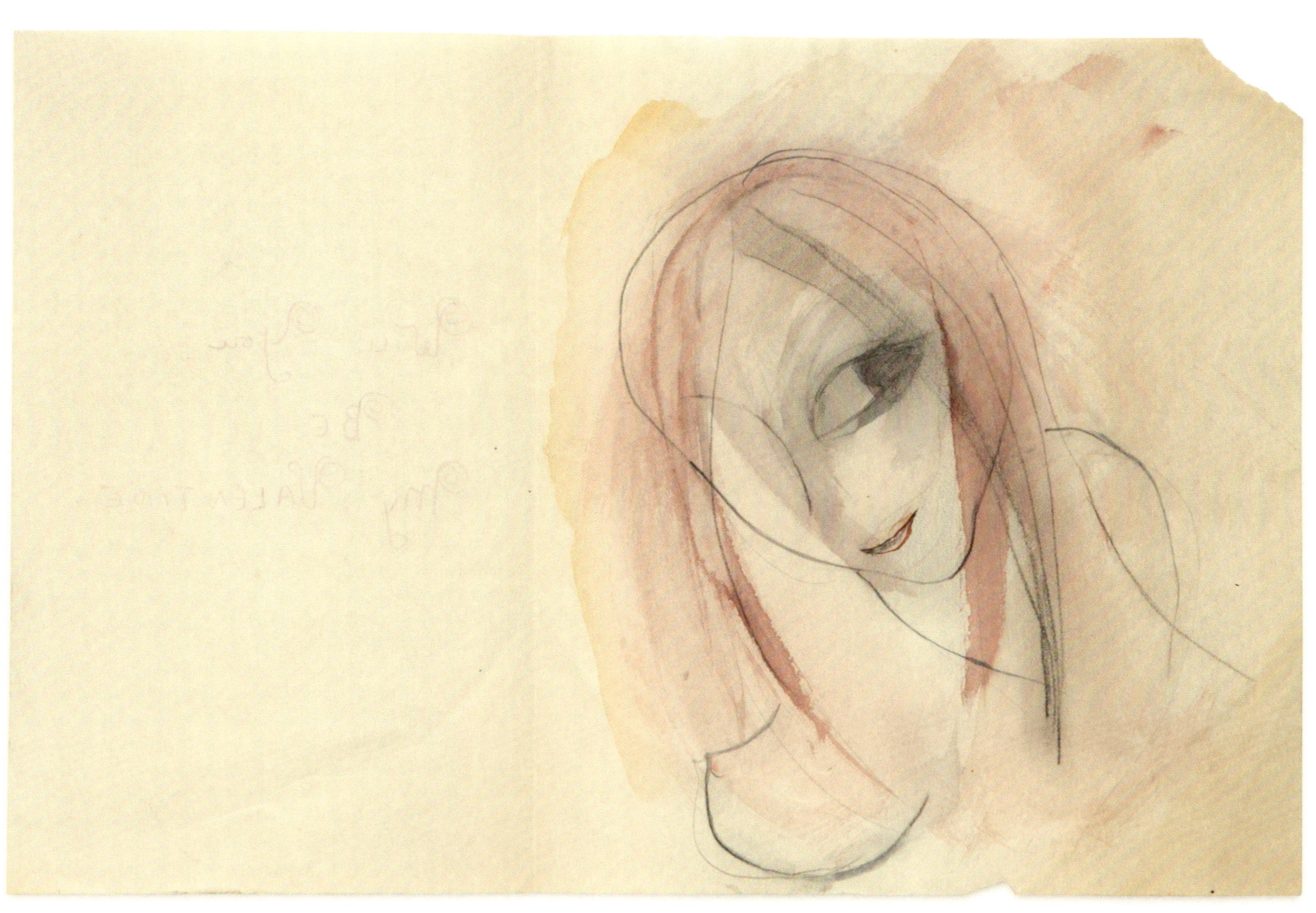

Untitled (4-page booklet), Undated, Illustration on paper, 6½ x 7¼" (folded), 6½ x 10½" (unfolded)

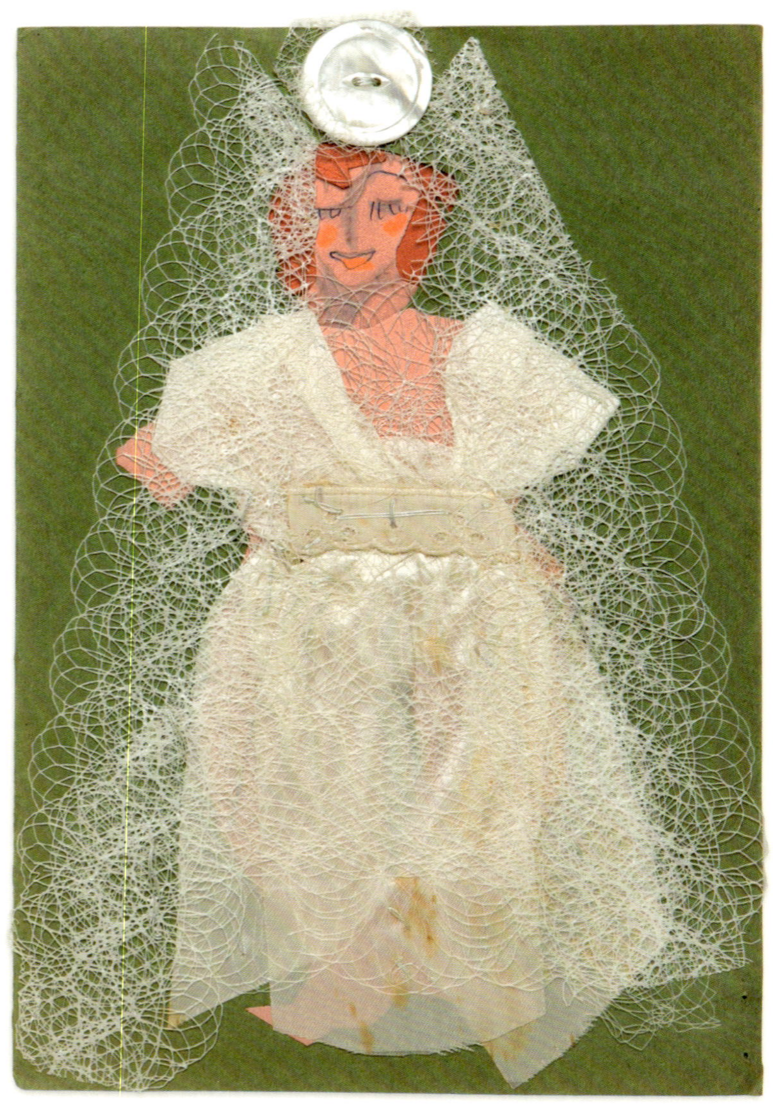

Could this be a play on Marcel Duchamp? The Bride Stripped Bare by Her Bachelors?

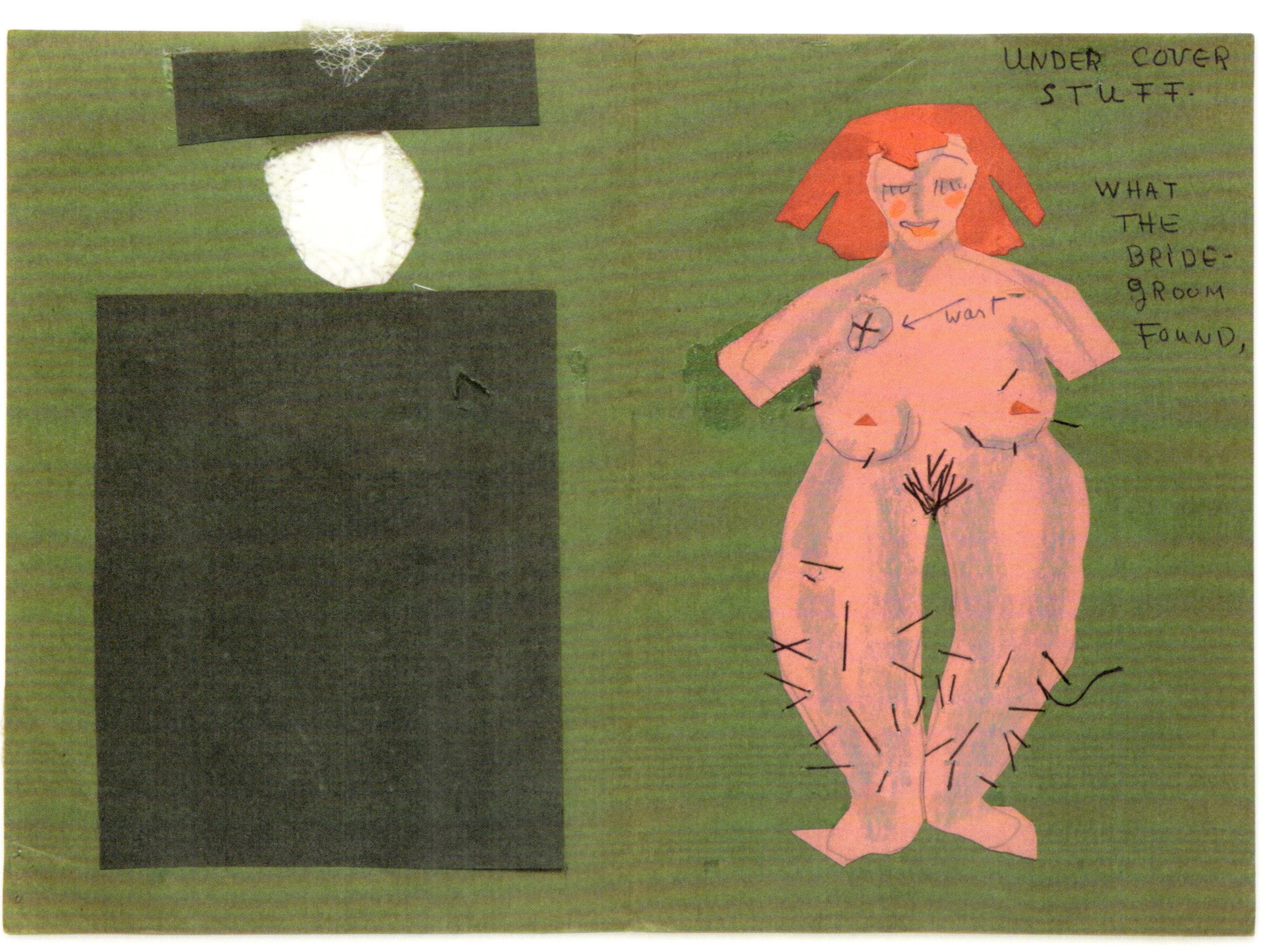

Untitled (4-page booklet), Undated, Paper and fabric collage, 9 x 6" (folded), 9 x 12" (unfolded)

"Steve wanted me To send This."

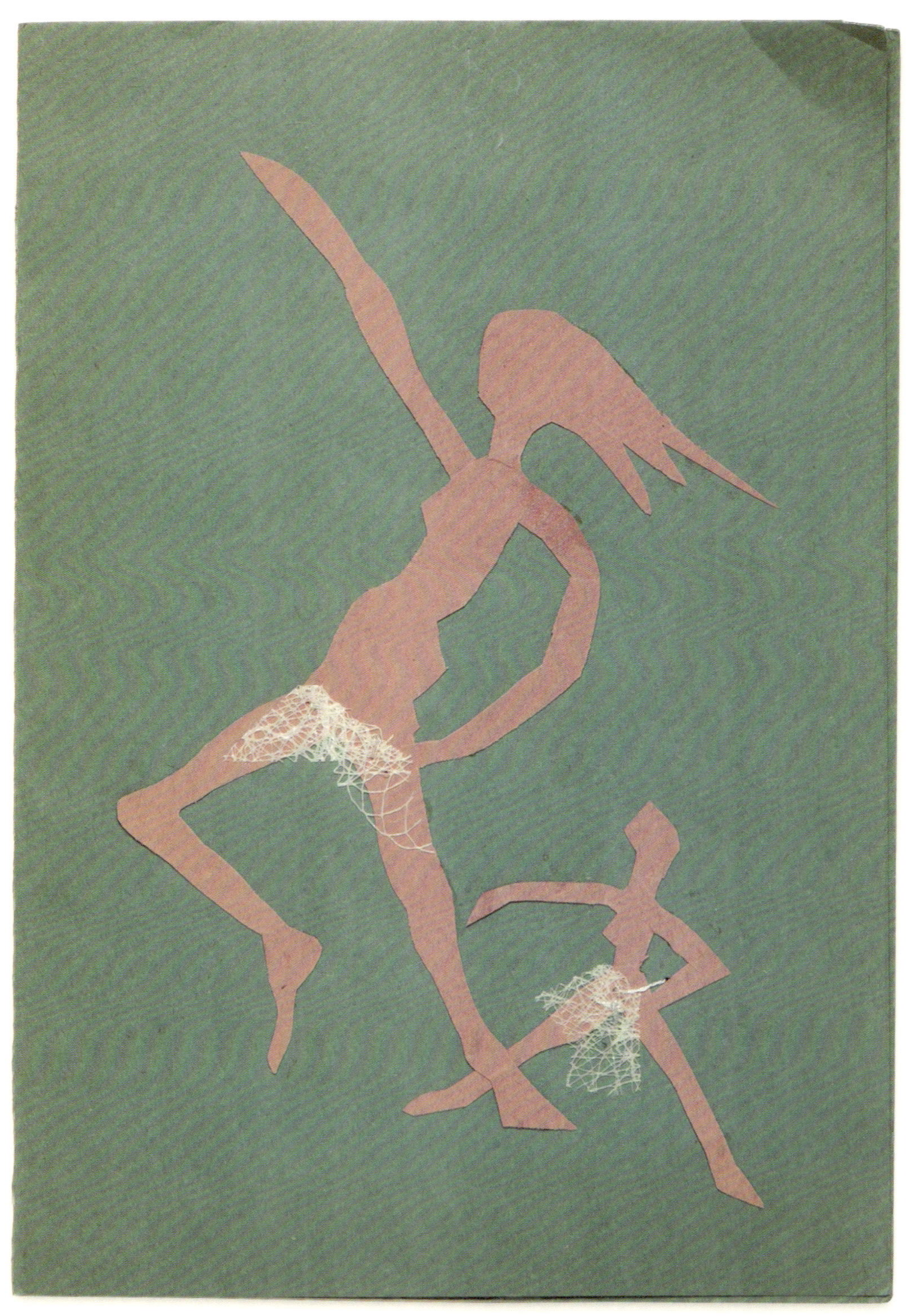

Untitled, Undated, Paper and fabric collage, 9 x 6"

"Will you be my Valentine? Please!"

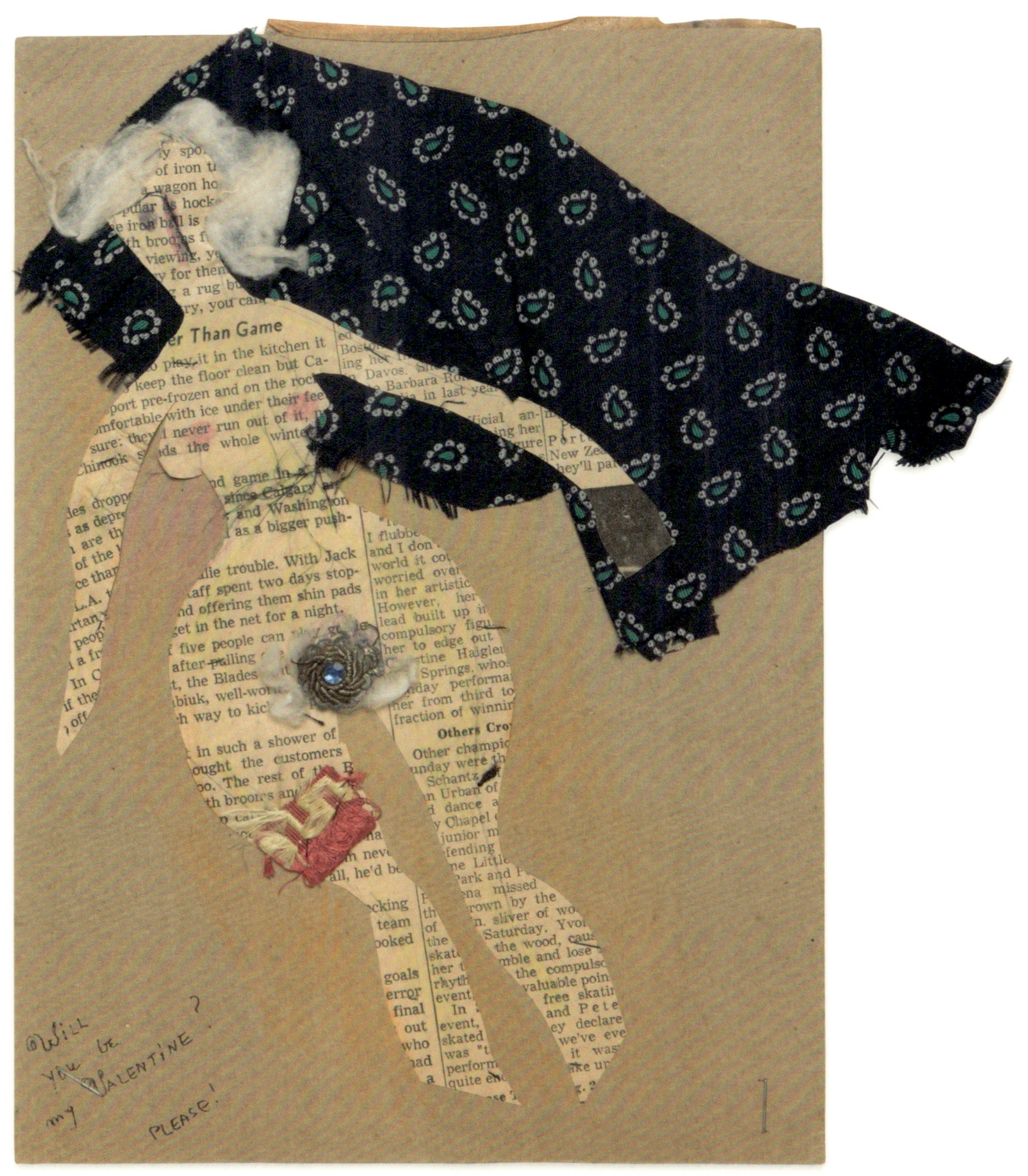

Untitled, Undated, Fabric, newspaper, and stones on cardstock, 10½ x 7½"

"WILL YOU BE MY VALENTINE:

Please straighten face"

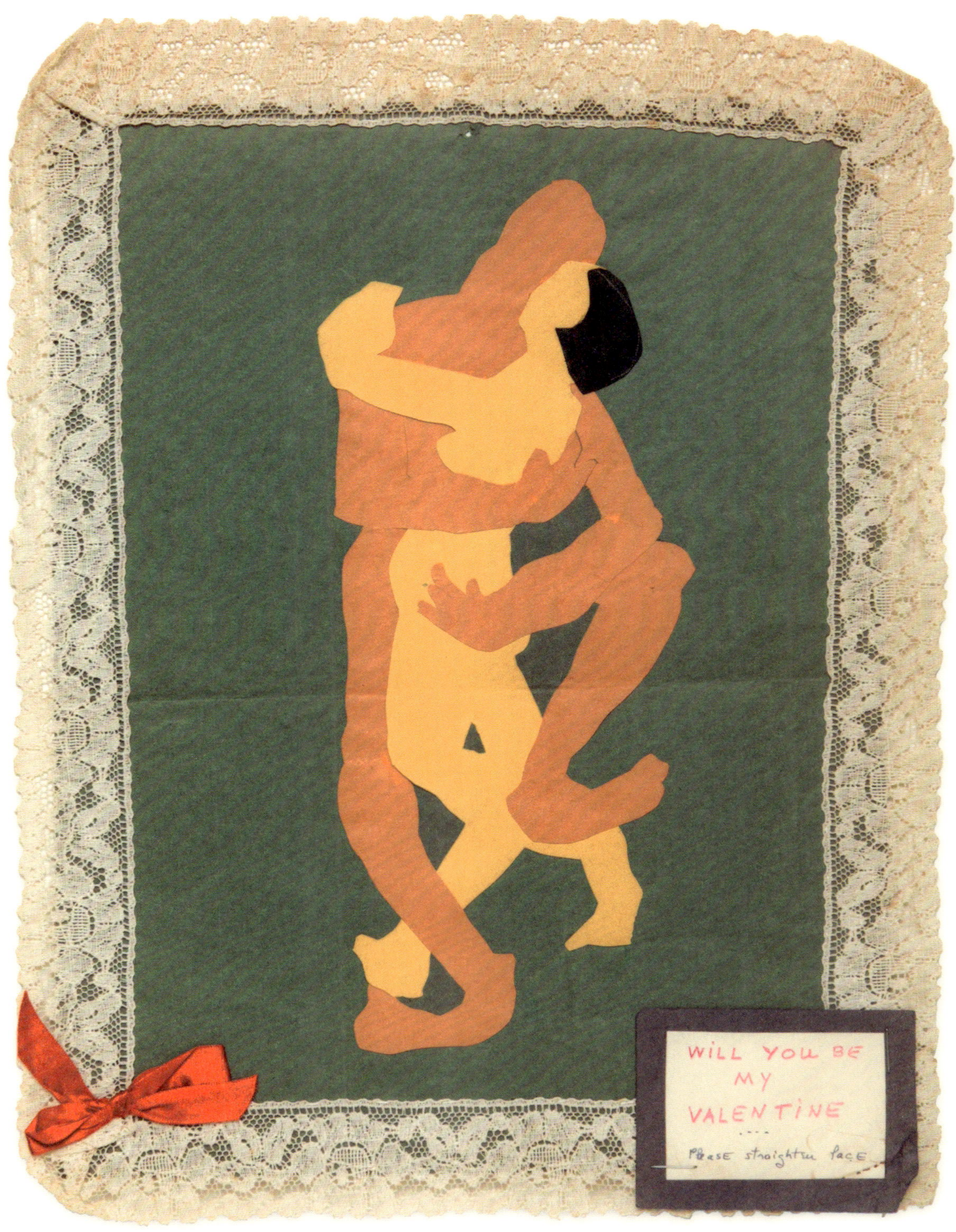

Untitled, Undated, Fabric, paper collage, 12½ x 10″

"CAREFUL! THE LEFT Bubby Still WORKS"

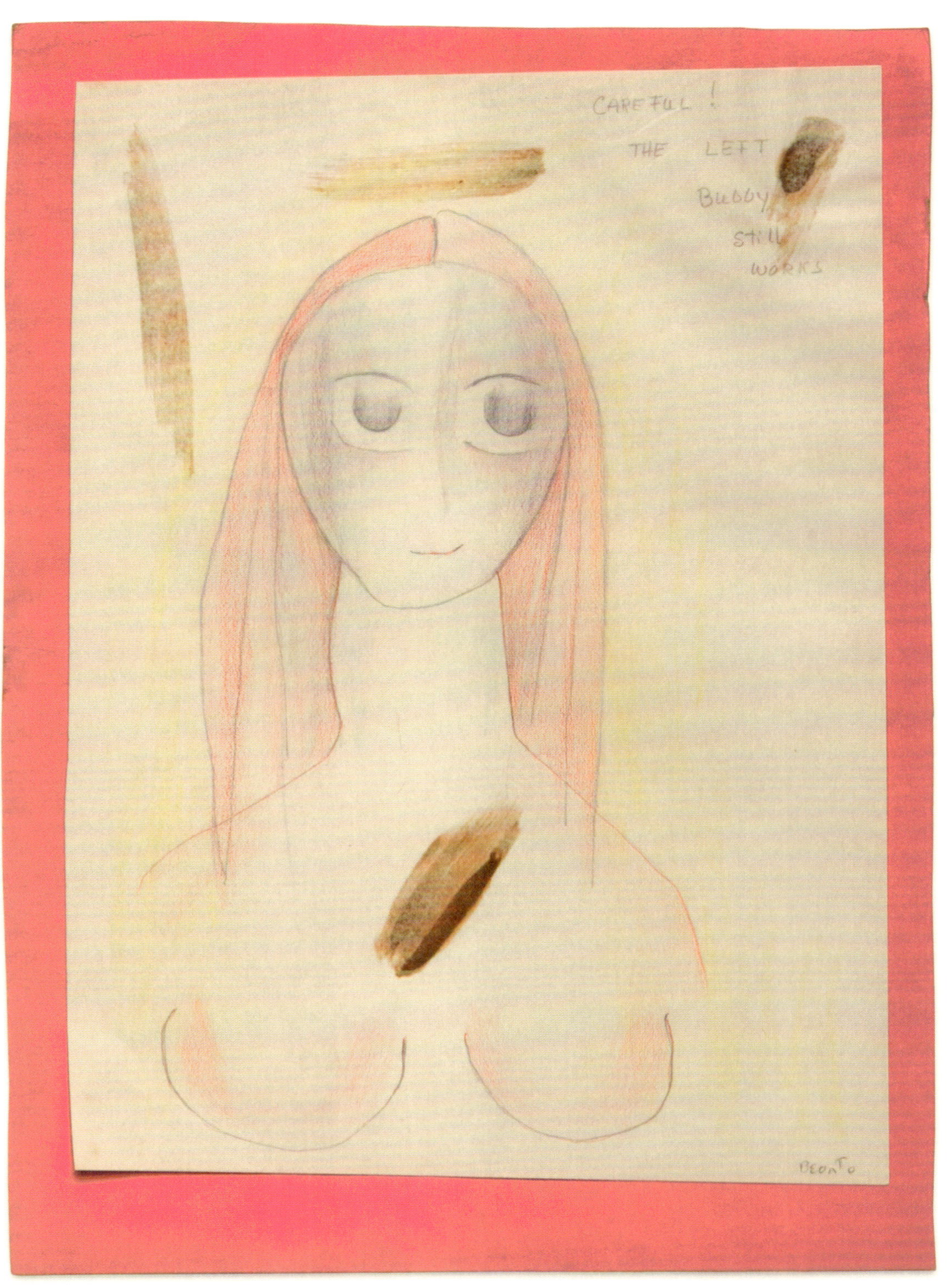

Untitled, Undated, Illustration on paper mounted on cardstock, 11¾ x 8¾"

"Rhea, Beato, Jack, Sonia

JACK TAKES OUT His CASTE iN THE SUN"

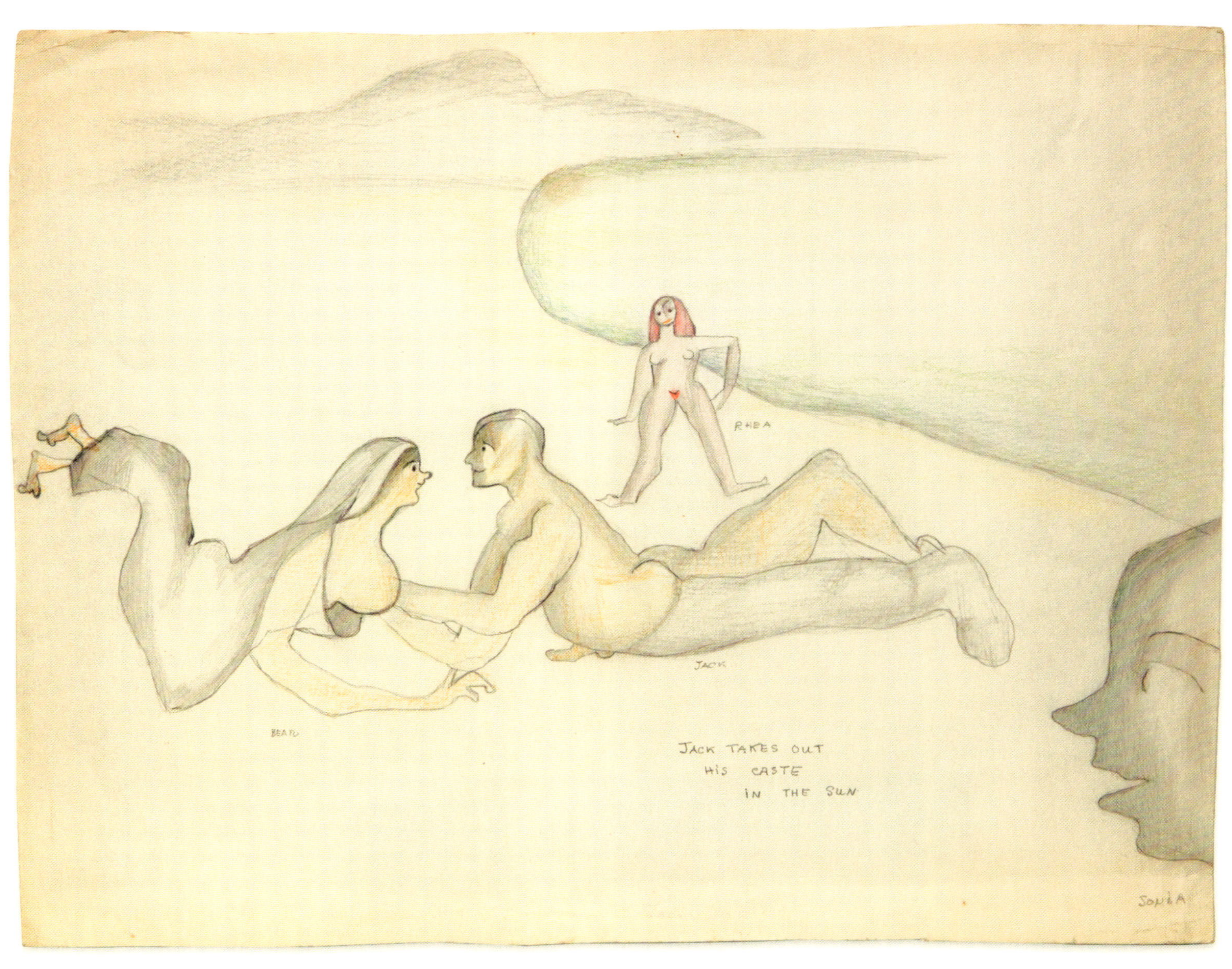

Untitled, Undated, Illustration on paper, 13 x 16"

"Hugs and Kisses—

Goodness sakes a mistake. This is meant for the nite!"

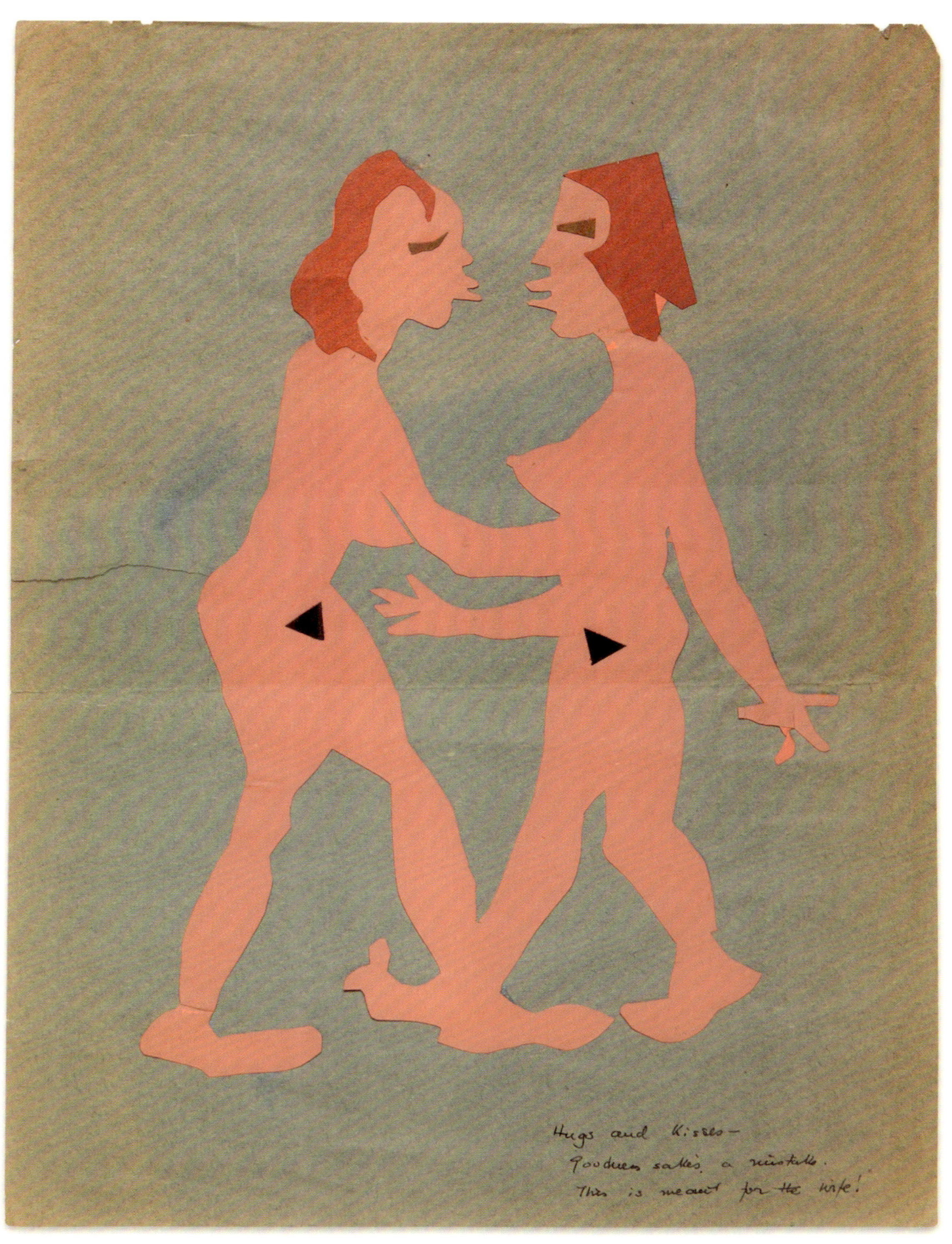

Untitled, Undated, Paper collage, 12 x 9"

For the garden

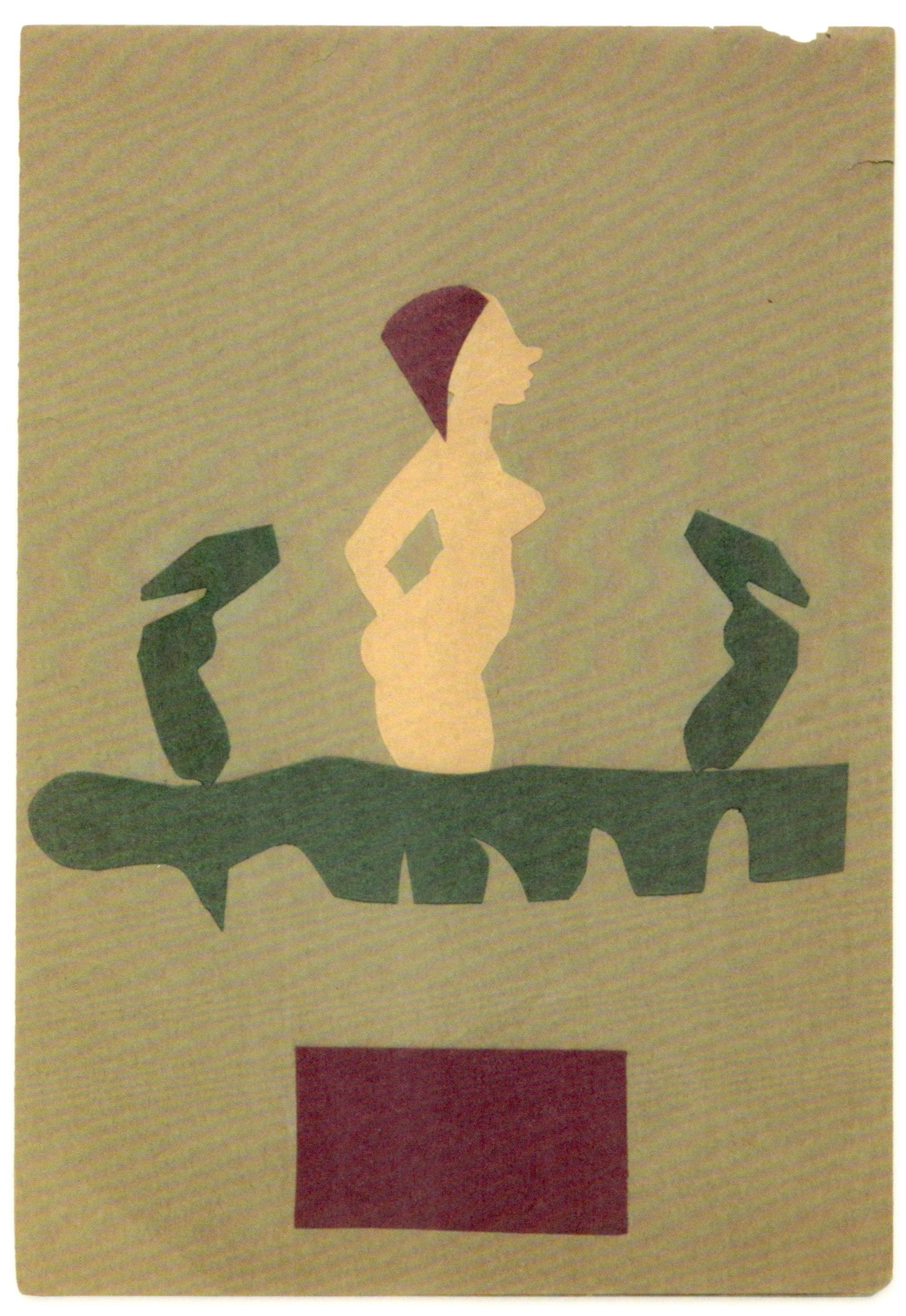

Untitled, Undated, Paper collage, 9 x 6" (folded), 9 x 12" (unfolded)

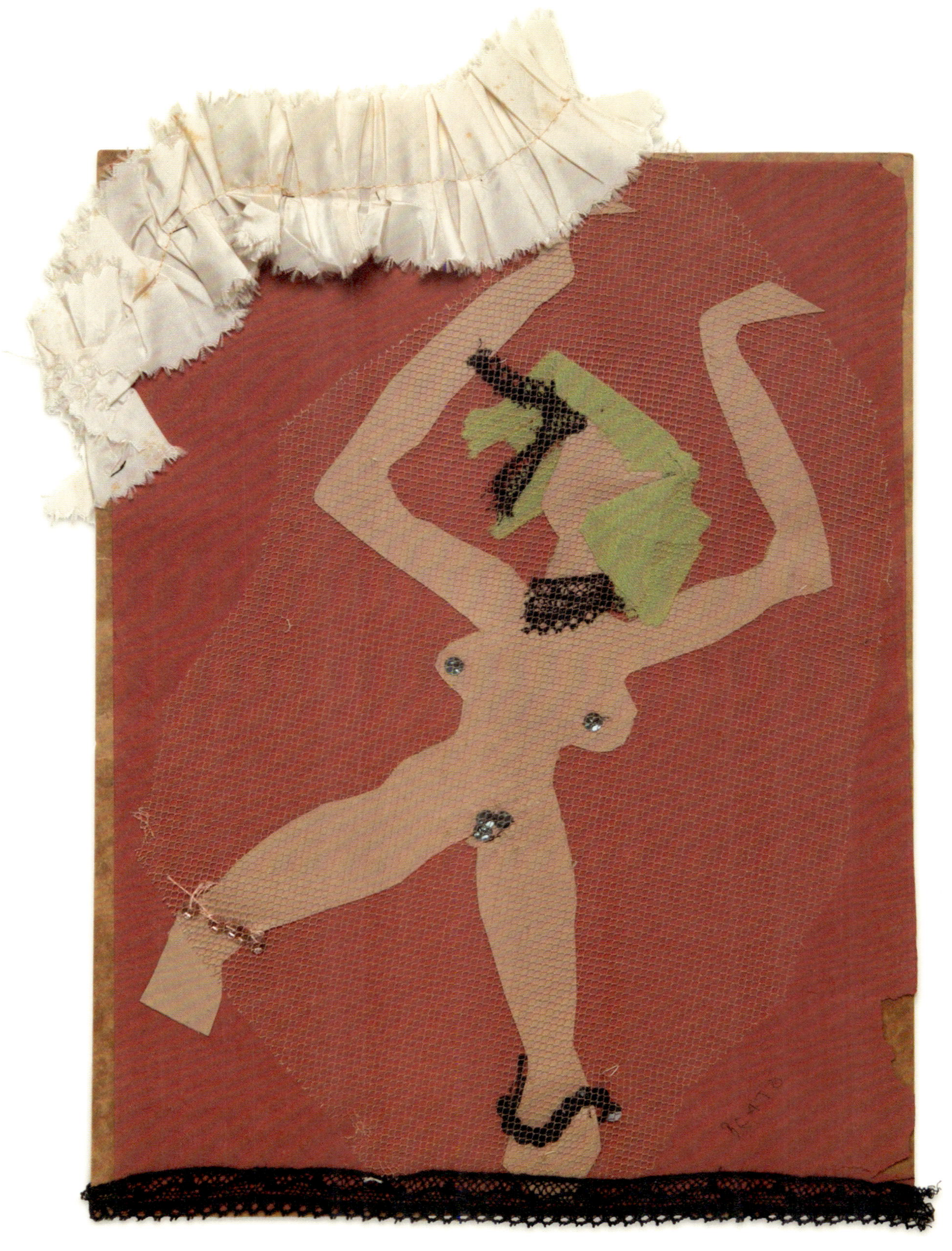

Untitled, Undated, Paper and fabric collage, 12 x 9⅕″

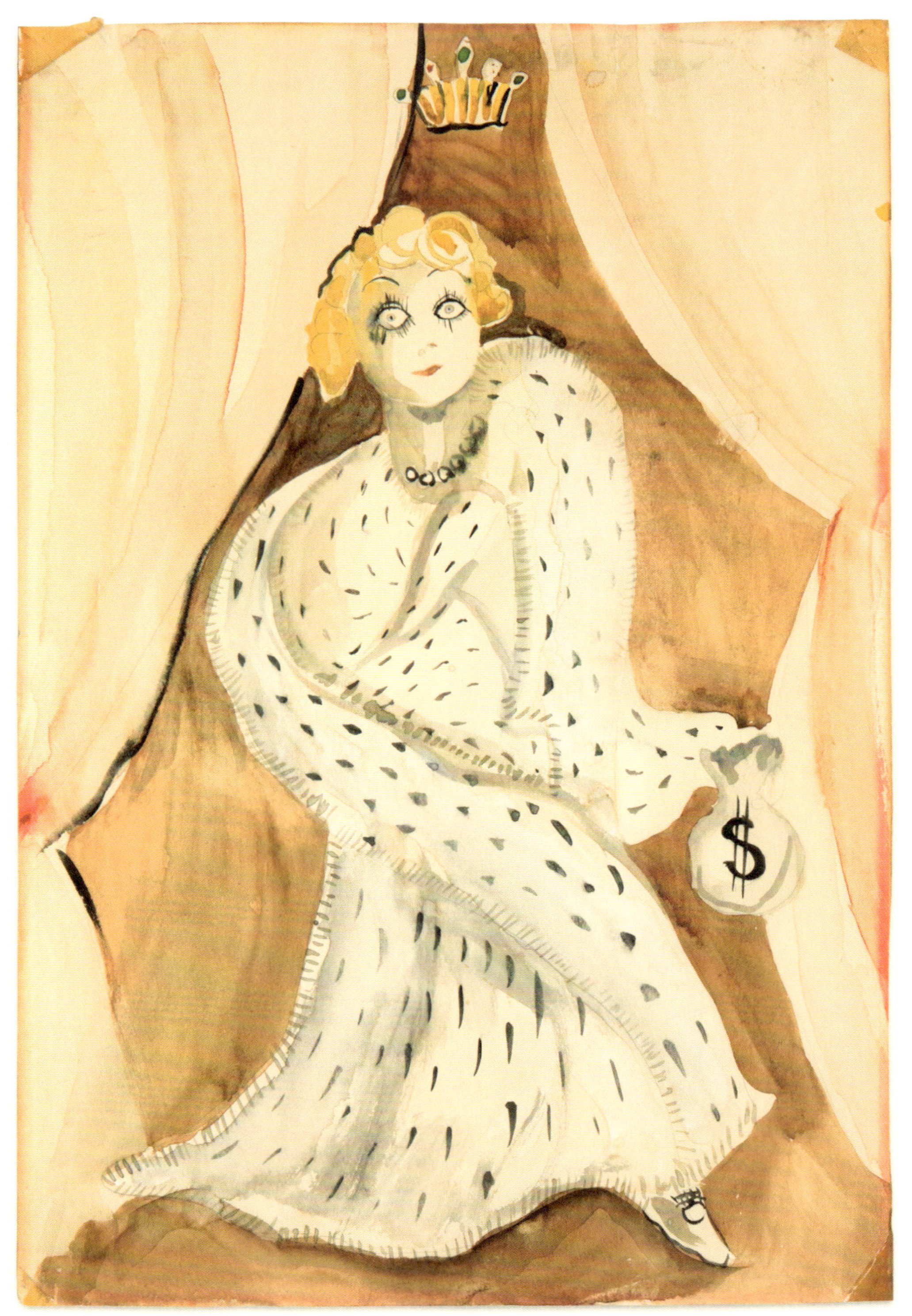

Untitled, Undated, Watercolor on paper, 17¾ x 11½"

"The dance of the Eighty nine positions.

This is the new game, in which the winner is he who can devise

the most change of posture. Very helpful for those who have rigititus in bed."

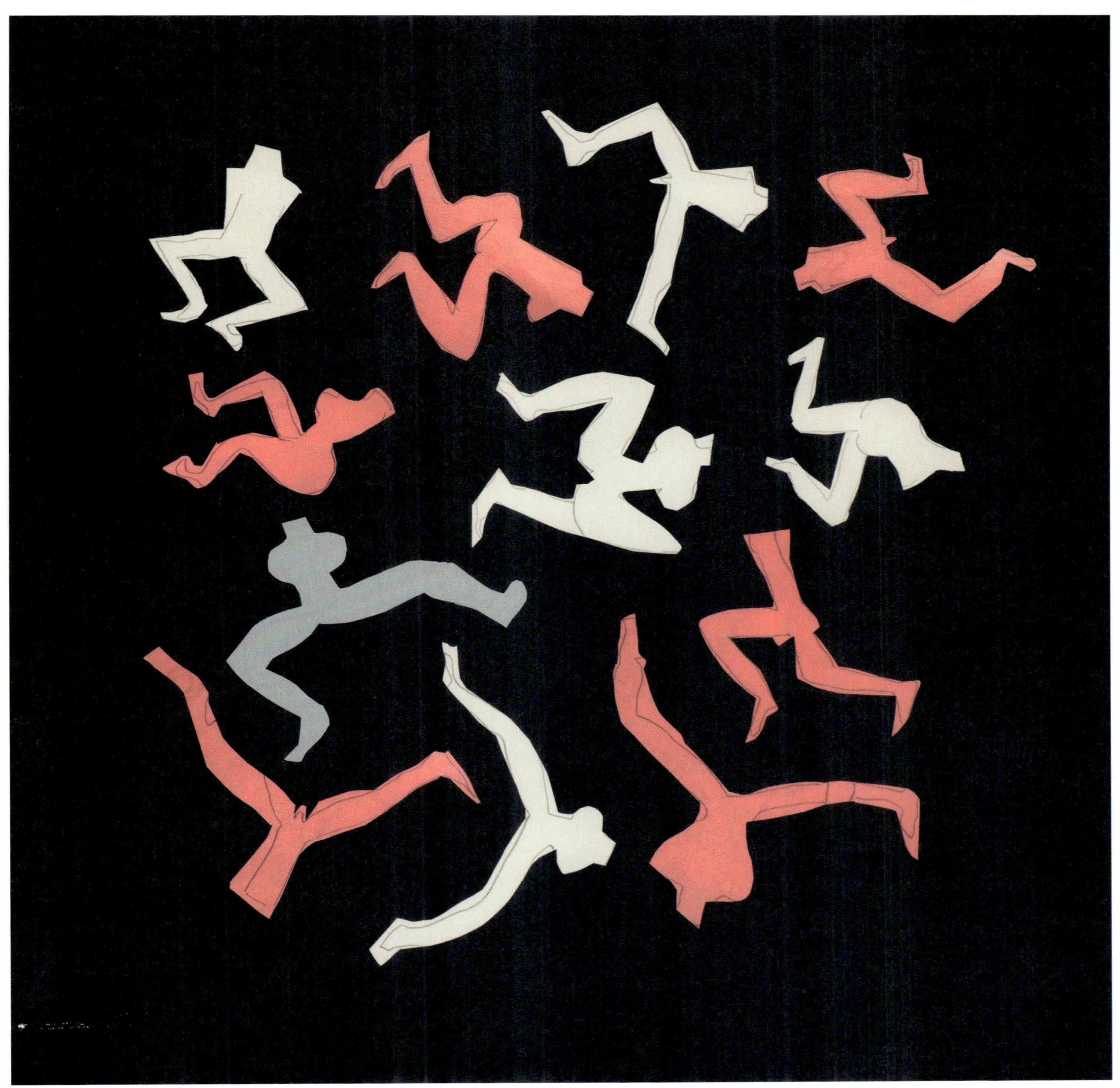

The dance of the Eighty nine positions, Undated, Paper collage, 11½ x 11½"

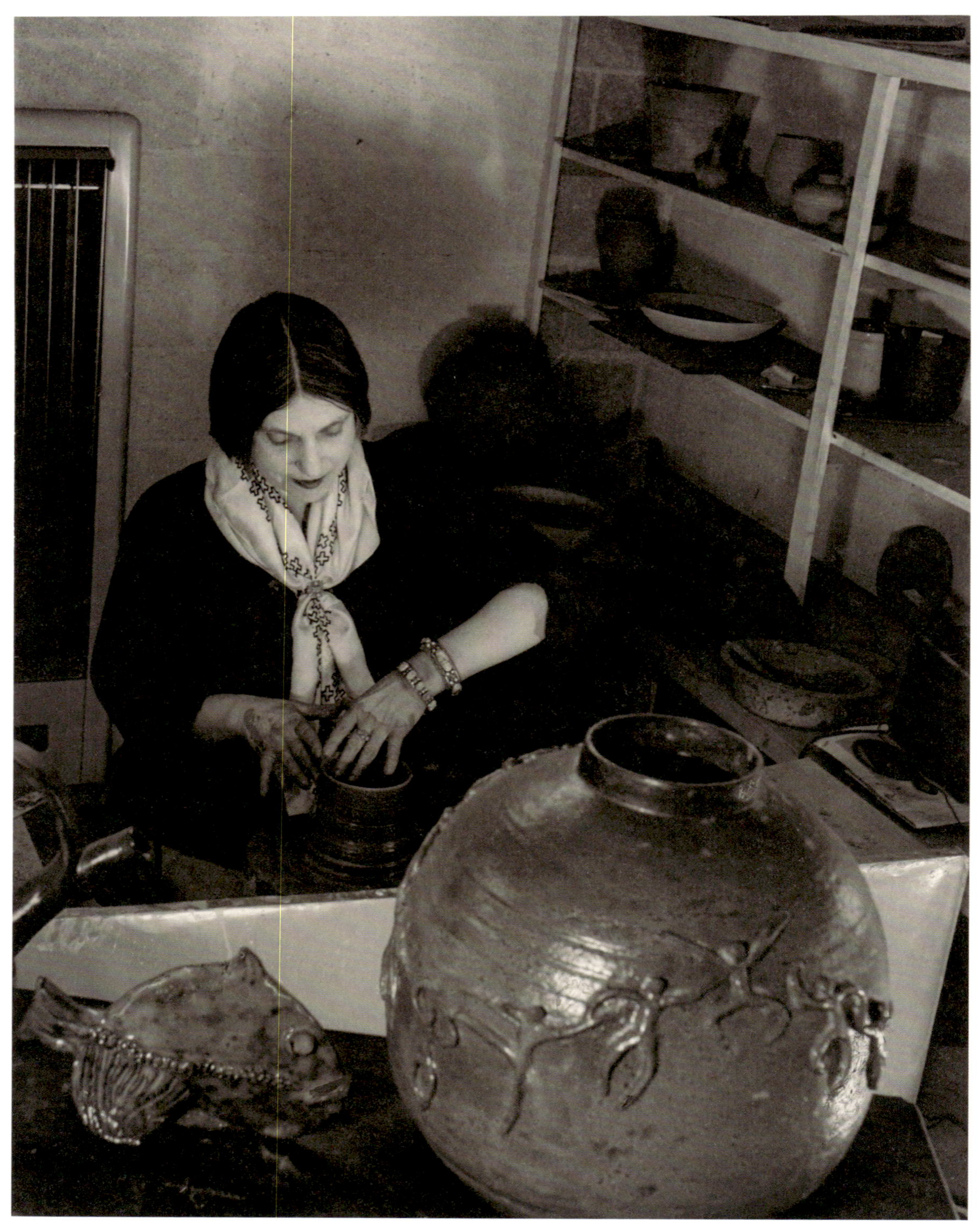

Jack Case, *Untitled* c. 1959, Silver Gelatin Print, from a scrapbook about Beatrice Wood
compiled by and in the collection of Rhea and Jack Case. It is captioned:
The artist is starting to throw a vase on a potter's wheel.

9   Beatrice Wood, *Lit de marcel* (Marcel's Bed). Pencil and watercolor on paper 8^1/$_8$ x 5^1/$_4$"
    Collection of Francis M. Naumann and Marie T. Keller. Photograph by Dana Williams.

10 *Untitled*, Undated, Illustration on cardstock, 15 x 10^3/$_4$"

11 *Evening at the Walter Arensbergs*, Undated, Illustration on paper, 9^1/$_4$ x 6^1/$_4$" "Marcel Duchamp, Walter"

25 *Untitled* (4-page booklet), 1934, Illustration on paper, 6^1/$_4$ x 5^1/$_2$" (folded), 6^1/$_4$ x 10^1/$_4$" (unfolded)

27 *Untitled* (4-page booklet), 1945, Paper collage, 6 x 6^3/$_4$ (folded), 6 x 13" (unfolded)

29 *Passion of Midnight*, 1949, Illustration on paper, 9^1/$_2$ x 12^1/$_2$"

31 *Untitled,* 1952, Work on paper, 13 x 9"

35 *THE CUT-THROAT WEDDING of Jack AND RHEA CASE—Oct. 1956*, 1956, Paper and fabric collage, 11 x 15^1/$_2$"

37 *Untitled* (2-page booklet), 1956, paint, paper and fabric collage, 18^1/$_2$ x 12" (folded), 18^1/$_2$ x 24" (unfolded)

41 *Untitled*, 1957, Paper and fabric sewn into a manila folder, 12 x 10" (folded), 12 x 20" (unfolded)

43 *Even Kinsey Blushed*, 1956, Paint, paper and fabric collage sewn into a manila folder, 11^3/$_4$ x 9^3/$_4$"

45 *Untitled* (4-page booklet), Beato's 1961 Valentine to Jack, Undated, Paper and fabric collage, 12 x 8^7/$_{10}$" (folded), 12 x 17" (unfolded)

49 *Untitled*, 1963, Paper and fabric collage, 10 x 7^3/$_4$"

51 *To Darling Jack and Rhea Case—Ojai—December, 1964*, Illustration, fabric, and paper collage, 12 x 9" (folded), 12 x 18" (unfolded)

53 *Untitled*, 1963, painting on paper, 14 x 16^3/$_4$"

55 *Untitled*, 1966, Paper and fabric collage, 12 x 18^1/$_2$"

57 *JACK CASE and His New Years Resolution*, Undated, Illustration on paper, 9^1/$_2$ x 12^1/$_2$"

58 *Untitled* (8-page booklet), Undated, Illustration on paper, 8^1/$_5$ x 5^1/$_2$" (folded), 8^1/$_5$ x 11" (unfolded)

61 *Untitled*, Undated, Paper collage, 10^1/$_4$ x 7^1/$_4$"

62 *Untitled*, Undated, Illustration on 4-fold paper, 4^1/$_2$ x 6^1/$_4$" (folded), 9 x 12^1/$_2$" (unfolded)

65 *Thank you for teaching me Japanese*, Undated, Illustration on paper, 12 x 8^3/$_4$"

67 *Oh, No, No. No!*, Undated, Illustration on paper, 12 x 9"

69 *Oh, YES, YES, YES!*, Undated, Illustration on paper, 12 x 9"

71 *WE ARE SO GLAD IT is ONLY YOUR TOE THAT iS BROKEN*, Undated, Illustration on paper, 16^1/$_4$ x 12^1/$_{10}$"

73 *Untitled* (4-page booklet), Undated, Illustration on paper, 6^1/$_2$ x 7^1/$_4$" (folded), 6^1/$_2$ x 10^1/$_2$" (unfolded)

74 *Untitled* (4-page booklet), Undated, Paper and fabric collage, 9 x 6" (folded), 9 x 12" (unfolded)

77 *Untitled*, Undated, Paper and fabric collage, 9 x 6"

79 *Untitled*, Undated, Fabric, newspaper, and stones on cardstock, 10^1/$_2$ x 7^1/$_2$"

81 *Untitled*, Undated, Fabric, paper collage, 12^1/$_2$ x 10"

83 *Untitled*, Undated, Illustration on paper mounted on cardstock, 11^3/$_4$ x 8 ^{3}/$_4$"

85 Untitled, Undated, Illustration on paper, 13 x 16"

87 *Untitled*, Undated, Paper collage, 12 x 9"

89 *Untitled*, Undated, Paper collage, 9 x 6" (folded), 9 x 12" (unfolded)

91 *Untitled*, Undated, Paper and fabric collage, 12 x 9^1/$_5$"

93 *Untitled*, Undated, Watercolor on paper, 17^3/$_4$ x 11^1/$_2$"

95 *The dance of the Eighty nine positions*, Undated, Paper collage, 11^1/$_2$ x 11^1/$_2$"

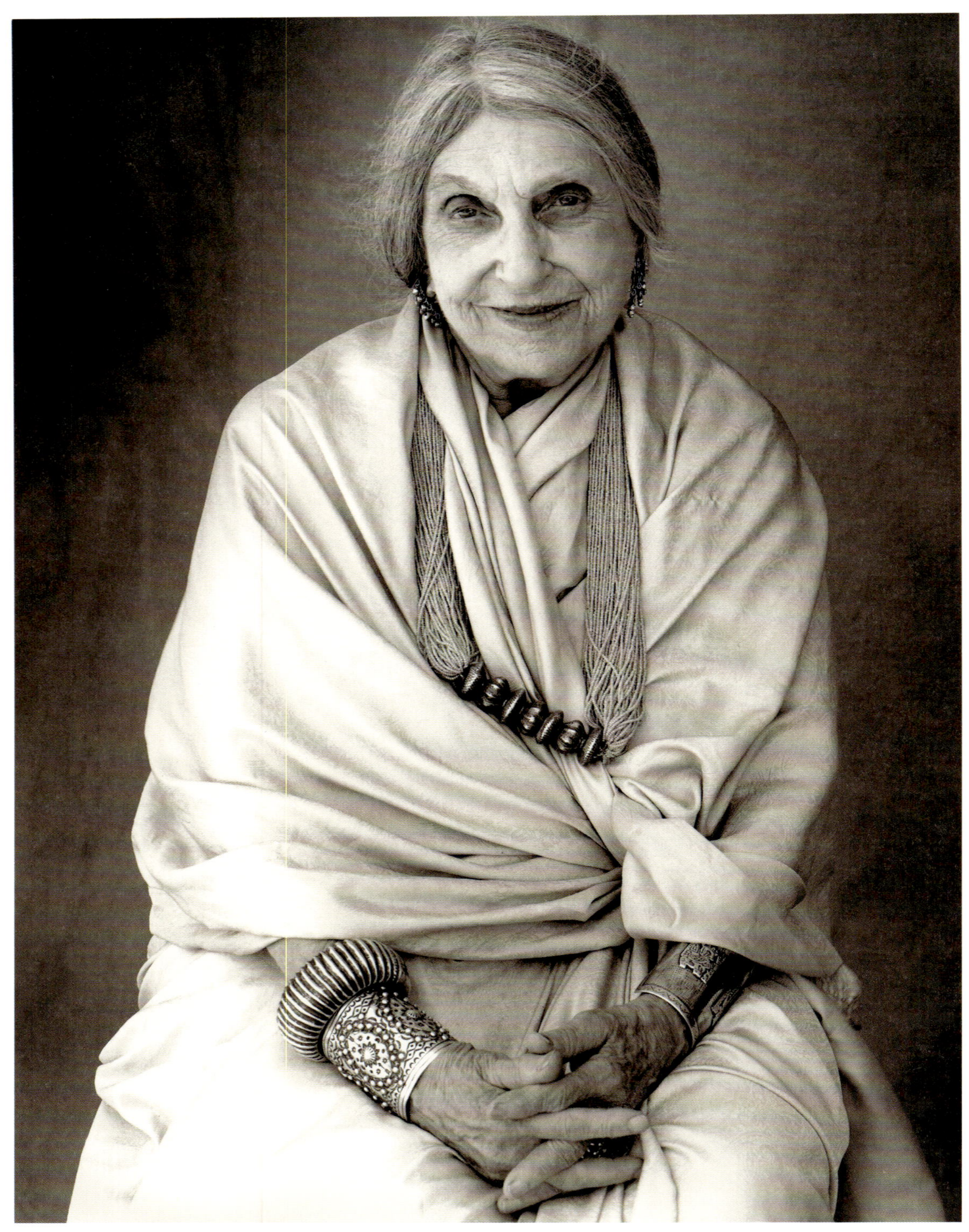

Anthony Cunha, Portrait of the Artist (Ojai California) Silver Gelatin Print, 1993.

ACKNOWLEDGMENTS

Many thanks to those who contributed time and talent to the compilation of this volume of drawings from the collection of Betsy and Marc Rowland: To FrescoBooks for a remarkable collaboration and your finesse, love, and sensitivity to the printed page, as always to Mark Del Vecchio, Marie-Claire Bryant, Gary Mankus Studios for digital imaging, Francis Naumann, and Dana Martin from the Francis Naumann Gallery, New York, Kevin and Sheryl Wallace from the Beatrice Wood Center for the Arts, and last but by no means least, the Archives of American Art, Washington D.C.

MÉNAGE
Beato

was printed by OGM, s.p.a. in Padova, Italy, on one-hundred-fifty gram GardaPat Klassika paper. The fonts used in the design were of the families ITC Avant Garde Gothic, Copperplate Gothic and Stemple Garamond. The print run consists of five hundred numbered copies: one hundred Collector Edition books housed in an Italian linen slipcase, and four hundred Special Edition books.

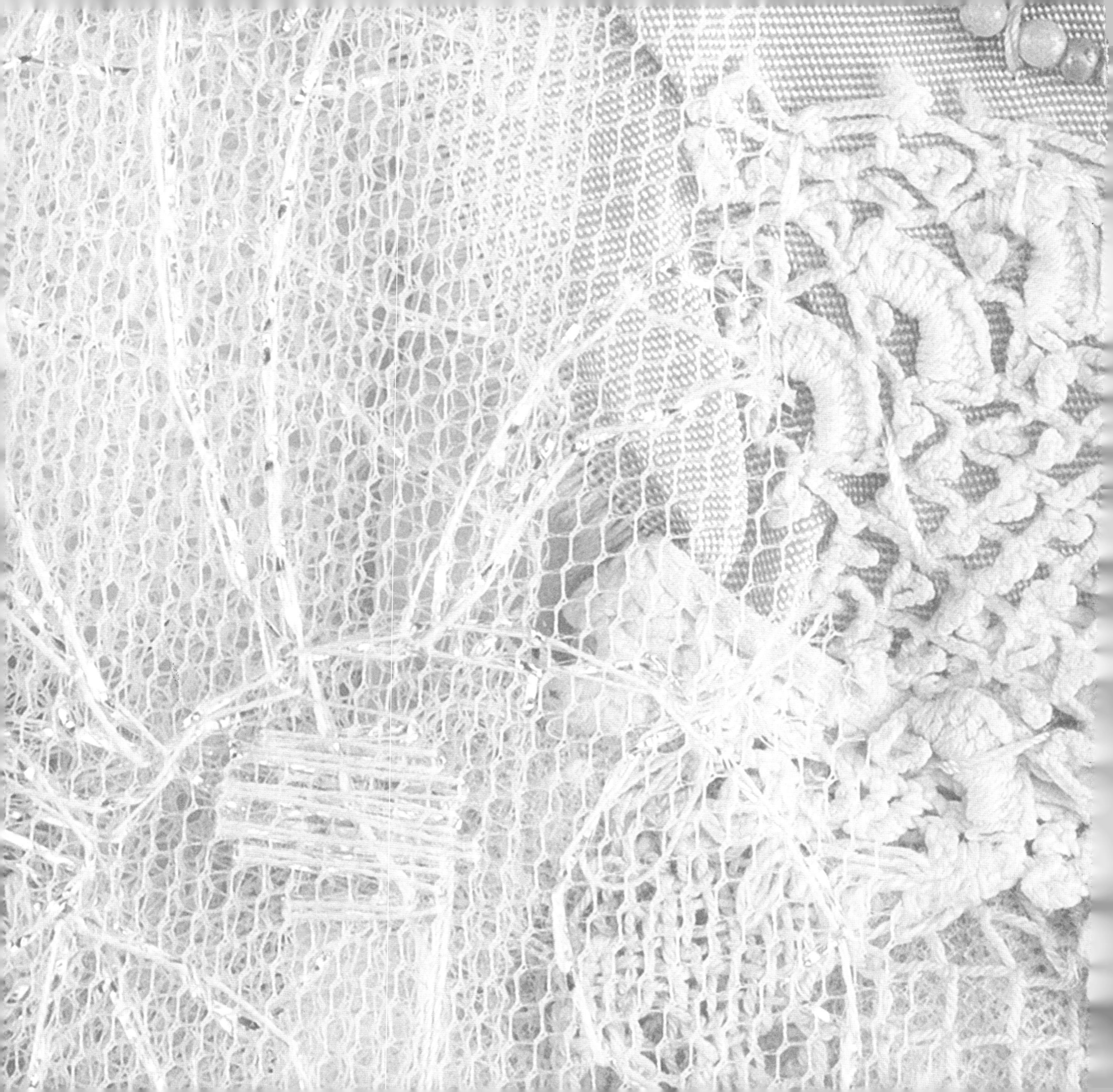